# Lost
# Masters

## Other Books by Linda Johnsen

*Daughters of the Goddess: The Women Saints of India*

*The Living Goddess:*
*Reclaiming the Tradition of the Mother of the Universe*

*The Complete Idiot's Guide to Hinduism*

Foreword by ECKHART TOLLE

# Lost
# Masters

## Rediscovering the Mysticism of the Ancient Greek Philosophers

## Linda Johnsen

• An Eckhart Tolle Edition •

New World Library
Novato, California

An Eckhart Tolle Edition
www.eckharttolle.com

New World Library
14 Pamaron Way
Novato, California 94949

Text design by Tona Pearce Myers

Library of Congress Cataloging-in-Publication Data
Names: Johnsen, Linda, [date] author.
Title: Lost masters : rediscovering the mysticism of the ancient Greek
  philosophers / Linda Johnsen ; foreword by Eckhart Tolle.
Description: Novato, California : New World Library, 2016. | "An Eckhart
  Tolle edition." | Originally published in 2006 by Himalayan Institute Press
  under title: Lost masters : sages of ancient Greece. | Includes bibliographical
  references and index.
Identifiers: LCCN 2016021275| ISBN 9781608684380 (paperback) |
  ISBN 9781608684397 (e-book)
Subjects: LCSH: Philosophy, Ancient. | Greece—Religion. | Yoga. | BISAC:
  BODY, MIND & SPIRIT / Mysticism. | PHILOSOPHY / History & Surveys /
  Ancient & Classical. | PHILOSOPHY / Eastern. | SELF-HELP / Personal
  Growth / General.
Classification: LCC B171 .J58 2016 | DDC 180—dc23
LC record available at https://lccn.loc.gov/2016021275

First New World Library printing, November 2016
ISBN 978-1-60868-438-0
Ebook ISBN 978-1-60868-439-7
Printed in Canada on 100% postconsumer-waste recycled paper

New World Library is proud to be a Gold Certified Environmentally
Responsible Publisher. Publisher certification awarded by Green Press
Initiative. www.greenpressinitiative.org

10   9   8   7   6   5   4   3   2   1

# Contents

# Foreword

ANCIENT GREECE IS RIGHTFULLY REGARDED as the cradle of European civilization. It produced unprecedented creativity and innovation in literature, painting and sculpture, politics, theater, architecture, and so on. The Greeks' most important contribution by far, however, consisted in what we might call an expansion of the abilities and scope of the human mind. They were able to free themselves from the constraints of culturally conditioned narratives, which millions of people are still trapped in to this day. These narratives are unquestioned beliefs and assumptions that are taken for reality. They are an intrinsic part of the conditioning of the mind. So one could say that the Greek philosophers taught us how to *think*. It is generally recognized, and taught at universities, that within the European cultural context, the civilization of ancient Greece gave rise to rational thought and ultimately laid the foundation for the development of science. This is all true, of course, but if that were the whole story, there would be no need for this book. It is not the whole story by any means. It is only one half of the whole. There is a dimension, which we could call spiritual, to these ancient philosophers' work that has been not only largely neglected by academic studies but actively suppressed. It is my view that their ability to think creatively and go beyond the confines of their mental conditioning was because they were able to access, to a greater or lesser degree, this dimension within themselves.

*Lost Masters* is all about this neglected but absolutely essential aspect in the lives and teachings of the great sages of European antiquity. If you are open to that dimension, you will want to read this book more than once. You will be amazed by the profound wisdom of these sages, which has been lost to us for two thousand years, except perhaps for a brief period when it was rediscovered in the Renaissance, only to be forgotten again.

The subject matter of this book is not just of historical interest. It is of vital relevance to our civilization at this time, which needs to rediscover its roots in that spiritual dimension if it is to survive, just as individuals need to discover that dimension within themselves in order to transcend the dysfunctional egoic state of consciousness that is the main source of human suffering.

The ability to *think*, which finds focused expression in the pursuit and ever-increasing expansion of scientific knowledge, is an amazing evolutionary attainment, but unless it is balanced with *awareness*, it becomes highly dangerous and destructive. The ego arises when there is complete identification with thinking without any background awareness. A person—or even an entire nation—then comes to be virtually possessed by certain patterns within the conditioned mind. When thinking and awareness are in balance, *wisdom* arises. Thinking then becomes fruitful and creative. The ancient philosophers were interested in knowledge, of course, and through the application of rational thinking, some of them arrived at astonishing insights. Democritus, for example, came to the conclusion (twenty-four hundred years ago!) that everything in the universe is made up of infinitesimally small particles he called "atoms," with empty space between them. Yes, the

Greeks were undoubtedly interested in knowledge, but more essentially they were interested in wisdom. That is why they called themselves "philosophers," which means "lovers of wisdom."

Wisdom arises out of awareness. Wisdom can manifest as thought, but the root of wisdom lies in "no thought," or freedom from thinking. That is why Socrates said: "Wisdom begins in wonder." What is wonder? The dictionary gives various definitions. The one that applies to the saying of Socrates defines *wonder* as "rapt attention or astonishment at something mysterious or new to one's experience." So when he speaks of "wonder," Socrates clearly refers to a state of alert inner stillness in which there is no thinking. There is awareness, but no narrative, no interpretation or explanation. This is corroborated by another one of his most famous, but usually misunderstood, sayings. When he was asked why the Oracle at Delphi called him "the wisest of all men" he replied: "I am the wisest man alive, for I know one thing, and that is that I know nothing." This statement is often interpreted as feigned modesty (which, of course, is a form of ego), but I would suggest that he was referring to the state of "not knowing" that precedes any creative use of the mind. In that state of alert inner stillness we connect with the unconditioned consciousness, so that we are no longer trapped in the conditioned mind. Plotinus puts it like this: "Leaving all thought behind, [the soul] releases itself into silence." The mind then becomes the instrument of a higher faculty instead of being self-serving, which is ego.

The state of consciousness that Socrates describes as "wonder" then prompted questions—questions that hadn't been asked before in the European cultural context: What is the nature of the cosmos? What lies behind the world that is accessible to us through sensory perception? What is goodness, virtue, love? Is there a Supreme Being? What is the optimal way for humans to live together? What are the ethical precepts for the conduct of our lives? And then they came up with answers, which were not definitive, and therefore didn't lead to dogmatic belief systems but remained provisional and explorative. This meant that there was always room to go deeper. The dictum "Know Thyself" inscribed at the temple of Apollo at Delphi pointed to the most important and profound question of all: Who am I? The answer to this question, of course, could not be a conceptual one, but would have to be experiential. Find the answer to this question, and it will transform you and your life!

We could say that the very prerequisite for any creative thinking is accessing the unconditioned consciousness within, which is the spiritual dimension. Discursive thinking becomes barren and even destructive when it has lost connectedness with that dimension. In other words, knowledge arrived at through rational thinking alone, lacking in awareness that engenders wisdom, is a dangerous thing, and the greater the knowledge, the more potentially destructive it becomes. These ancient sages knew that the most important task for us humans is conscious connection with the spiritual dimension. Virtue, love, right action, and creative thinking arise from that. It is the essence of who we are. Hence Pythagoras taught: "People run in every direction meeting sorrow after sorrow. Why? Because they're disconnected from themselves." So knowledge is important, but wisdom is primary. The ancient Greek sages were primarily teachers of wisdom. Although they were seekers of knowledge, the greatest of them were ultimately aiming at the transformation of the human being, which means the transformation of human consciousness. Although the knowledge they gained laid the foundation for science, most of them had more in common with the traditional Indian gurus than with modern-day scientists or academic philosophers. Indeed, an important feature of this book is the clear and plentiful evidence it presents to show that many of the Greek sages were aware of and influenced by the spiritual teachings and practices of the older cultures of Egypt and, more importantly, India.

Despite the fact that there is undoubtedly a collective spiritual awakening happening on our planet, affecting a certain, as yet relatively small, percentage of the total population, there is at the same time an intensification of egoic unconsciousness and dysfunction that could well lead to increasing collective insanity, resulting in violent upheavals, destruction, and the rapid demise of our civilization. The poet W. B. Yeats wrote the famous line: "Things fall apart; the centre cannot hold." I would suggest that the problem is not that the center cannot hold, but that humans are unaware of the center, unaware of their innermost essence, which is the spiritual dimension of life. When millions of humans live in that state of unawareness, attempting to find an ever-elusive satisfaction in sensory gratification and material things, they give rise to a civilization that is "like a house built on sand, without a foundation," to paraphrase the words of Jesus.

Then there is no true transcendent value to hold the civilization together anymore, and "things fall apart." Cleverness and even "intelligence" in the conventional, "IQ" sense of the word are not enough to hold a civilization together or to bring true fulfillment to a person's life.

As you read this book, you will find that the long-lost masters, who lived in a distant past when the world was young and whose most essential teachings were forgotten or suppressed, are coming back to life within you. As you read this book, you will not only embark on a journey back in time to the very origin of our civilization but you will also find yourself on a journey without distance into the timeless dimension of who you are.

—ECKHART TOLLE, author of
*The Power of Now* and *A New Earth*

# Lost Masters Timeline

The dates of spiritual masters born before the fifth century C.E. are rarely certain, whether they were born in the East or the West. Many of the dates listed here are guesses based on scanty or conflicting evidence.

## Before the Common Era

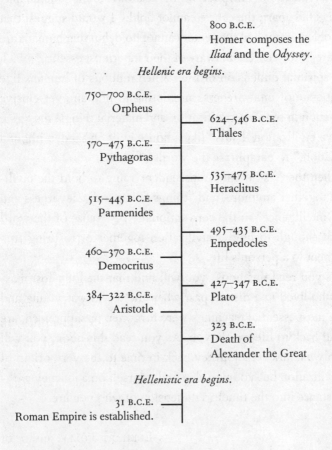

800 B.C.E.
Homer composes the *Iliad* and the *Odyssey*.

*Hellenic era begins.*

750–700 B.C.E.
Orpheus

624–546 B.C.E.
Thales

570–475 B.C.E.
Pythagoras

535–475 B.C.E.
Heraclitus

515–445 B.C.E.
Parmenides

495–435 B.C.E.
Empedocles

460–370 B.C.E.
Democritus

427–347 B.C.E.
Plato

384–322 B.C.E.
Aristotle

323 B.C.E.
Death of Alexander the Great

*Hellenistic era begins.*

31 B.C.E.
Roman Empire is established.

## Common Era

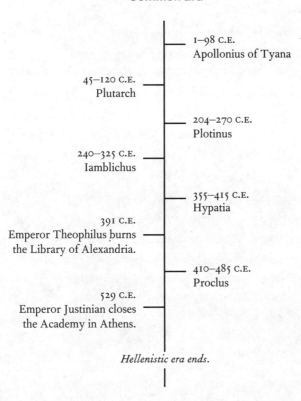

1–98 C.E.
Apollonius of Tyana

45–120 C.E.
Plutarch

204–270 C.E.
Plotinus

240–325 C.E.
Iamblichus

355–415 C.E.
Hypatia

391 C.E.
Emperor Theophilus burns
the Library of Alexandria.

410–485 C.E.
Proclus

529 C.E.
Emperor Justinian closes
the Academy in Athens.

*Hellenistic era ends.*

# CHAPTER ONE

# The Light of the West

NO ONE READS THE ANCIENT GREEKS anymore. In the last century scholars accomplished something no literate person in past ages could have imagined: they made the Greeks *boring*. I slept through my Ancient Western Philosophy class in college, resentful that my Jesuit professor inflicted the dialogues of Plato and Aristotle's outdated metaphysics on defenseless freshmen like me.

It would be decades before I realized the Greeks were neither dull nor irrelevant—in fact, until the modern period, Plato was recognized as one of the greatest mystics in the history of Western civilization, and Plotinus (who carried on Plato's tradition five hundred years later in Rome) towered over the centuries as a giant of Western spirituality. These men were not just thinkers—they were considered sages, transmitters of a profound and inspired wisdom tradition that paralleled the mystical lineages of India. As late as the Renaissance, the stature of the ancient Greek philosophers as spiritual masters of the first magnitude was acknowledged throughout the Christian and Islamic worlds.

I didn't have a lot of patience for the Greeks. Like many children of the 1960s, I turned to the Hindu Upanishads not Plotinus' *Enneads* for enlightenment, to India's *Ramayana* and

*Mahabharata* not Greece's *Iliad* and *Odyssey* for inspiration, and to Krishna and Buddha rather than Homer or Socrates for heroes. Compared to Hindu seers and Buddhist siddhas, the much-vaunted Greeks seemed like lightweights.

Ironically, it was my Indian researches that led me back to Greece. I learned that a Greek magus named Apollonius of Tyana had visited India in the first century c.e. and that a fairly detailed account of his travels had actually survived. Reading Apollonius' story was a galvanizing experience, revealing astonishing connections between the Greek, Roman, Egyptian, Persian, and Indian cultures, which most modern historians neglect. My interest in the Greek thinkers was piqued: How did it happen that many of their doctrines and religious practices matched the teachings of the Indian sages so closely? Was Apollonius correct when he claimed that the Greeks had learned their doctrines from the Egyptians—and the Egyptians learned them from India?

So I returned to the Greeks, reading the portions of Plato my Jesuit professor had advised us students to skip. Sure enough, there was the juice, the living spirituality that so appalls academics today but kept the greatest minds of the Western world enthralled for more than a thousand years.

I went back to the original Greek historians, such as Herodotus, Diogenes Laërtes, Diodorus Siculus, and Plutarch, in an effort to learn what the ancients said about their own tradition before modern scholars reinterpreted it for them. I was continually amazed at how similar the long-lost Greek world was to the India I travel through today, where the perspective of the ancients still lives in Bengali villages and Varanasi enclaves and the palm jungles of Kerala. The type of spiritual practices that Plotinus— perhaps the greatest of all the Hellenistic masters—described in his *Enneads* are as much alive in Himalayan caves today, where Plotinus is unknown, as they are moribund in American and European universities that claim to teach Plotinus!

It's surprising that today yoga students can read Plotinus and instantly recognize the higher states of consciousness he was describing, correlating them point for point with the levels of meditative focus listed in India's *Yoga Sutras* in 200 B.C.E. Yet Western scholars often ignore these very passages! They represent "Oriental contamination" of the pure Greek tradition, my professor claimed. And he was right—you can find Eastern influence throughout Greek thought.

I was so flabbergasted by the correlations between the Greek and yogic traditions that I started telling everyone I knew about the ancient Western sages. My friends would get as excited as I was and insist, "This information is incredible! It's unbelievable we haven't heard about this before. You've got to write a book." So here it is.

I very much want to introduce you, too, to the great spiritual masters of our past, Western "gurus" whose traditions, unfortunately, we've forgotten. Their life stories, like those of sages everywhere, are remarkable. And their distinctive approaches to spirituality will remind you of similar Hindu, Buddhist, yogic, and tantric lineages. They do differ from Indian gurus in many important respects, of course. India was a much older and far more sophisticated culture. Yet the differences aren't as great as you might imagine. The "mystery religions" that so inspired Greek and Roman civilization were also clearly related to the wisdom of India, especially in their doctrines of karma, reincarnation, and spiritual transcendence.

## The Hellenes

Let me say a few words here about the region of time and space covered in this book. The Hellenic and Hellenistic epochs were a period of astonishing intellectual advances dominated by the

Hellenes, as the Greeks called themselves. The Hellenic era lasted from about 800 B.C.E., when the poet Homer is said to have composed his brilliant epics about the early Greek heroes who built the Trojan horse, to around 336 B.C.E., when Alexander the Great (the student of Aristotle, who was in turn the student of Plato) first leaped onto the world stage.

The Hellenistic era began with Alexander, who spread Greek culture as far west as Afghanistan. His conquests stopped only when his men refused to go farther, recognizing the futility of attempting to conquer India. This era in one sense ended around 31 B.C.E. with the birth of the Roman Empire. In another sense it continued through about 500 C.E., when Christian rulers shut down the Hellenistic universities. Till then most educated people still wrote in Greek, and the Greek worldview held sway over Western consciousness. In this book I will introduce you to some of the greatest spiritual masters of the full Graeco-Roman period, from the Hellenic era through the sixth century C.E.

The "Greek" scientists and philosophers, artists, and sages didn't just come from Greece, by the way. Some of the greatest were from Turkey and Egypt, Italy and Bulgaria, Sicily and Syria. "Greece" at this time was more a state of mind than a physical location.

I believe bringing the viewpoint of the East to our knowledge of ancient Greek culture will vastly enrich our understanding of our own spiritual roots as Westerners. But first we need to know what those roots are. In reclaiming our ancient European heritage, we reconnect with the living spirituality at the heart of our civilization, a tradition that speaks to us more urgently than ever as we "New Age" foundlings search for authentic spiritual experience.

I believe the time has come to resurrect the ancient Greek masters, to hear again their perennial wisdom, and to live once more the ageless truths of the active spiritual life they embodied.

# CHAPTER TWO

# The Mystery Religions

On September 21, 1962, Robert Paget and Keith Jones discovered the entrance to hell. They found it right where classical Greek and Roman authors had always said it was, in the volcanic fields along the western coast of Italy—ironically, not far from the Vatican.

The two retired naval officers lowered themselves cautiously into a passage hidden beneath an ancient temple complex at Baia. They'd been warned they might be killed instantly by poisonous gases, but the air was just barely breathable. Stumbling down a long, narrow tunnel for about 400 feet, marked with niches where ancient priestesses had set oil lamps, they came to the "parting of the ways" where the tunnel split into two separate shafts, an important feature of hell described in ancient texts. By this point the temperature had risen to 120 degrees Fahrenheit. In another 150 feet the explorers were stopped dead by gurgling volcanic waters. They had reached the shore of the River Styx.

In 1870 Heinrich Schliemann astounded the world when he took the fables in the *Iliad*, Homer's ancient Greek epic, seriously enough to follow their trail to the ruins of Troy. Troy was supposed to be a myth, not a real city that had actually presided over the Hellespont, where the Mediterranean greets the Black Sea. Here the amateur archaeologist unearthed what many today believe to be Homer's defeated city, which perhaps really did fall to the jealous fury of Menelaus and Agamemnon long, long ago, as the Greek poet had claimed.

But even Schliemann could hardly have imagined that Hades—the dark cavern of the afterlife where Homer's heroes ultimately found themselves—might really exist. Yet in Homer's *Odyssey* the sorceress Circe described the sea route to Hades in specific geographic terms that seemed too detailed to be mythical, to Robert Paget's literal way of thinking. Other ancient writers such as Virgil and Pausanias had described the site as if it were a physical location, and Livy mentioned that no less a luminary than Hannibal—the African general who drove elephants over the Alps to menace the Italians—had paid his respects at the oracle there some twenty-two hundred years ago. It hadn't sounded to Paget like these classical authors were making it up. With tireless enthusiasm, and with what must also have seemed to their friends like embarrassing naïveté, he and Jones followed the crumbs dropped by writers of antiquity to this hole in the ground in the Phlegrean fields southeast of Rome.

In the archaeological flurry that followed Paget and Jones's discovery, experts agreed the two explorers had indeed uncovered "the Oracle of the Dead," the entrance to Hades visited by such Greek and Italian heroes as Odysseus and Aeneas in the hazy beginnings of European history. Suddenly it no longer seemed so odd that the poet Virgil had described hell in such minute detail in his *Aeneid*. He had no doubt stopped there many times—he lived just a few miles away.

"Hades" remains one of the most enigmatic archaeological finds of the twentieth century. The site is undatable; it must have existed in Homer's time since his description of both the shrine and its environs is so accurate, suggesting the site goes back to at least 800 B.C.E. If Odysseus really did visit it, as Homer claimed in the *Odyssey*, it must date back to Mycenaen times, perhaps 1200 B.C.E. It could in fact be far older—Paget suspects it was constructed sometime during the Stone Age. Its sacred purpose is immediately evident: the first section of the tunnel, 408 feet long, is oriented directly toward sunrise on the day of the summer solstice. The inner sanctuary, where Odysseus spoke with the ghost of the sage Teiresias, is oriented toward the sunset.

But what is so puzzling is how Hades could possibly have been built in the first place. Incredibly, a 200-yard subterranean passage heads directly toward an underground stream of boiling water 150 feet beneath the surface of the Earth, as if its planners knew exactly where to find "the River Styx." No false starts or exploratory excavations have been located: the workers, digging or drilling through solid volcanic rock, knew exactly where they were going. Engineers today would be hard-pressed to locate an underground hot spring so accurately.

The construction of this underworld is a marvel. The shape and dimension of its galleries were designed with painstaking precision, the tunnels measuring 6 feet tall by 21 inches wide. The ventilation system is quite sophisticated and would pass an engineering inspection even today. The temperature and water level of the boiling volcanic springs at the bottom of the complex remained constant till the day Paget scrambled inside, still regulated by mechanisms put in place by the original builders thousands of years ago.

So much about this rock-hewn Hades remains a mystery. What we know for sure is that sometime during the reign of Caesar Augustus, Marcus Agrippa (Caesar's right-hand man) was dispatched to close the gates of hell. At his order 19,000 cubic feet of earth were hand carried into the complex to fill the northern shaft.

Given that only one man could pass through the narrow tunnel at a time, the work must have taken years. Then immense 20-foot-long blocks were set in place to seal the tunnel forever. Whoever wanted the entrance to hell shut down must have wanted it *very* badly. An earthquake—probably the enormous temblor of 63 C.E.—partially sealed the rest of the site until our two indefatigable naval officers lowered themselves in almost exactly nineteen hundred years later.

Over the long centuries a temple to the wisdom goddess Minerva continued to operate at the surface of the Oracle of the Dead, but eventually the underground sanctuary was forgotten, and Hades faded into the shadows of mythology.

## The Oracle of the Dead

What on earth were the ancients doing in this carefully carved pit? Scholars today speculate it was an immensely successful business concern, a sort of ghoulish Disneyland. Oracles go back a long way in the old world, and the Mediterranean was peppered with them. There was money to be made from people's fears, then as now, and pretenders to supernatural knowledge rarely suffer from a lack of paying clients.

The scenario scholars have worked out runs something like this. Clients showed up at the temple complex overlooking the Gulf of Baia frightened, confused, desperate, or recently bereaved. They may have been in trouble with the gods, like Odysseus, or could have had problems with powerful relatives, like Hercules, who was ordered to pillage the site by his vengeful uncle. Aeneas, legendary father of the Roman people, was sent to our oracle by the famous Sibylline prophetess from nearby Cuma, who was undoubtedly paid a handsome kickback for the referral. The Sibyl explained this was the one spot on earth where someone who was not already dead was allowed to enter the world beyond—provided, of course, they brought a generous offering for Persephone, goddess of that gloomy underworld, and for the priestesses and priests who served her there. In the netherworld one could reconnect with a parent or spouse who had passed away, seek counsel from a respected seer of yore, and receive assurance of the soul's survival after death, even if this meant souls lived on in the damp and dismal cavities of the earth.

Each new client fasted and prayed, keeping all-night vigils in the temple of the grim goddess on the bay. Drugs were slipped into his drink, and once he was in a sufficiently hallucinatory frame of mind, dark-robed priests sent their terrified customer into the dark corridor leading down toward his tryst with the dead. Knees knocking, the visitor descended into the earth, accompanied by appropriate sound effects (the shrieks and moans of temple staff) to the boiling river below. As he neared the end of this short but petrifying journey, he glimpsed the departed soul he sought to contact, or rather a carefully coached priest or priestess standing in for the deceased, in a confusing billow of smoke and light. The customer would ask his questions, hopefully receive the guidance and reassurance he had come for, and then rush back up the tunnel, grateful to reemerge in the land of the living. It was a glorious fraud, brilliantly conceived and thrillingly executed. Some of the greatest heroes of ancient Greek culture were completely fooled.

Is this what was *really* going on at the Oracle of the Dead? Maybe—but maybe not. I would like to suggest an alternative scenario.

Thanks to advances in medical science, thousands of critically ill patients have survived to report a near-death experience. Called back from the dead—resuscitated after having been declared legally dead following an accident or surgery—these individuals allege, in remarkably similar terms, that they felt a disembodied version of themselves floating through a long, dark tunnel, where they encountered a being of light who helped them review their past life and future destiny with a profound sense of clarity and joy. Many report returning to their bodies completely transformed by the experience.

Whoever built Hades seems to have constructed it with the near-death experience in mind. If you had visited the Oracle of the Dead two thousand years ago, you would have walked down a long, straight tunnel toward a distant light, the sacred fire burning in the inner sanctuary at the bottom of the passage. But on your way you had to make a choice: the tunnel divides in two, one tube leading directly to the bright light, the other to the boiling water below. Remarkably, this underworld geography illustrates one of the oldest images in mystical literature. Already in the *Rig Veda*, the Bible of India composed more than five thousand years ago, you were warned that after death you must decide which of two paths to follow: *devayana*, literally "the way to the light," or *pitriyana*, "the way to the ancestors." The first path was said to lead to higher states of consciousness in worlds beyond our own. The second involved crossing a river the Hindus call Vaitarani, meeting friends and relatives who had passed on before you, and ultimately returning to embodied life in the physical world.

*Vaitarani* means "difficult to cross." If you "drown" in the Vaitarani, you are swept back into the material world and "die" into a new physical body. Your memory of your previous life is erased by a force the Hindus call *vaishnava shakti*. If instead you choose the path to the light, you are reborn among the stars. Instead of forgetting the past, you retain your identity, yet with vastly expanded awareness. Ancient Egyptian funerary paintings reflect the same imagery: tombs show recently departed souls hoping to avoid a crocodile poised to drag them down into the river of death, and focusing their attention instead on the stars painted above them. In fact, in advanced meditative states, intense starlike points of light, called *bindus* in Sanskrit, are often reported.

Because of its obvious connection with the after-death imagery of many spiritual traditions, it's tempting to speculate that the Oracle of the Dead may originally have been designed as a mystery school, where novitiates were initiated into the secrets of life after death. We know that Egyptian hierophants, Tibetan lamas, Hindu yogis, and Jewish and Christian gnostics memorized instruction manuals meant to help them navigate the next world. Some of these remarkable texts still exist. Ancient Greek writers often refer in deeply respectful tones to the mystery schools of their own day, where the hidden truths of birth, death, and the conquest of death were taught. The teaching wasn't verbal as it is in our educational institutions today. Instead inner experiences of the soul were acted out, enabling initiates to experience these hidden truths viscerally. Walking down that dark tunnel in Italy to directly confront one's deepest fears, pre-enacting one's own journey after death, may have been the most powerful transformative experience the preceptors of the Stone Age could devise. I would imagine it was an incredibly effective exercise!

## The Light in the Tunnel

What was really going on in the Oracle of the Dead at Baia? Initiations into the ultimate mysteries of human life or cynical manipulation of bereaved clients, misled into believing they could contact the dead? Perhaps both, at different times in the long history of the site.

We are told, however, that the priests and priestesses who served there never saw the light of day. They spent their entire lives in the dark confines of the Oracle, coming outside only at night. It's hard to believe deliberate frauds would impose such severe penance on themselves. Perhaps the priest who embodied Teiresias for Odysseus truly believed he was speaking for a soul who had gone on before, just as mediums and channels believe they do today. Maybe through sacrificing outer light they genuinely hoped to glimpse the light within. (This type of spiritual discipline was still attested well into the twentieth century. For example, specially selected Kogi children in Columbia were raised in continuous darkness by tribal elders with the expectation that in this way their inner vision would develop fully. BBC reporters in South America have taped remarkable film footage of this training program.)

What we know for sure about the mystery religions is that the central human issues of death and rebirth lay at their core. They addressed the adventure of consciousness as it cycles in and out of bodies, back toward itself, the light at the end of the tunnel.

The influence of the mystery religions on ancient Greek and Roman civilization was immense. Whole segments of their populations were initiated in the schools of the Earth Mother, Demeter, or of Dionysus, the god of wine. Isis' mysteries spread from Egypt as far north as Britain and, according to one Egyptian papyrus, as far east as India.

Many embraced the tradition of Magna Mater, the "Great Mother" imported from eastern Turkey. In some respects Magna Mater eerily resembles the Hindu goddess Durga (also called Sri Mata and Maha Devi, "Great Mother" in Sanskrit). Her priests in Rome practiced rites identical to those celebrated by Durga's priests in northwestern India. Back in Turkey Magna Mater was called Truqas, a name etymologically linked with Durga, and was commonly pictured with a lion, just like Durga. Magna Mater was an important goddess in Western history; she became the chief deity of the city of Rome around 204 B.C.E. and was worshiped there for five hundred years. Her mysteries symbolized the relationship of the Sun and Venus on one level, and of the Supreme Spirit and human soul on another.

The religion of Mithras, related to the Sun god Mitra of India's *Rig Veda*, was practiced in dark underground rooms called *mithraea*, designed to look like caves. The mithraea were decorated with images of the signs of the zodiac as well as the constellations of the celestial equator. Recently researchers have shown that at least some of the stunning Paleolithic paintings on the cave walls of Lascaux in France were unmistakably astronomical. This raises the possibility that cave initiations meant to guide the soul to palaces in heaven may have been practiced in Europe for twenty thousand years.

The famous Eleusinian mysteries also were celebrated, in part, in cave-like enclosures. There the descent of the virgin goddess Persephone (representing the soul) into Hades and her reemergence from the land of the dead were ritually reenacted. Some Christian scholars have noted that Jesus' tomb was probably a cave. To this day Indian yogis spend long retreats in caves, seeking spiritual rebirth or practicing *kaya kalpa*, the ancient yogic technique of completely rejuvenating one's body.

## Rising from the Dead

In the Roman myth, Persephone was captured by Pluto, king of the underworld, which represented the physical world "underneath" the higher, formless world of spirit. Through the intervention of the Divine Mother, she could have escaped quickly, but she had made the mistake of eating a bit of food in Hades. It was a *really* small bit—the seed of a pomegranate—but that was enough for Pluto to insist that Persephone had accepted his hospitality and so must remain in Hades as his wife. To yoga students today, as to initiates in the Greek world, the implications were clear: when the soul desires the fruit of the material world, it becomes trapped in the wheel of reincarnation, being born and dying and being born again as inexorably as the seasons follow each other. Adam and Eve, you'll remember, also got into trouble when they tasted the fruit.

Ultimately, Persephone rises gloriously from the land of the dead into real life, the life of spirit. This vision of the risen Persephone was the culminating experience acted out in the Eleusinian mysteries. Scholars have long speculated what this vision must have entailed. In India to this day, during a rite called *devi bhava*, a human woman surrenders her limited awareness to the Great Goddess and becomes the vehicle through which the Goddess's grace is physically transmitted to her devotees. Having witnessed this rite many times, I can honestly report that the numinous sense of blessing power the incarnate Goddess conveys can be truly staggering.

Let's turn now to one of the most mysterious and influential Western traditions of all. It was founded by a complex and enigmatic figure, the prophet and musician the Greeks called Orpheus. This astonishingly yogi-like adept can barely be glimpsed through the mists of prehistory, yet his effect on early Western civilization, and later on Christianity, would be profound. He is the first of the ancient sages you're about to meet.

# CHAPTER THREE

# Calming the Savage Heart

ORPHEUS

MANY OF US VAGUELY REMEMBER ORPHEUS from the little bit of Greek mythology we learned as children. He was the lyre player who climbed down into Hades (perhaps the very same Hades Paget and Jones explored) in a futile attempt to bring his bride, Eurydice, back from the dead. His poignant music so deeply moved the gods of the underworld that they agreed to allow Eurydice to leave—provided that as Orpheus led her out of the earth, he didn't look back. It's not hard to guess what happened next. At the last moment Orpheus reflexively glanced backward to make sure his wife was still behind him. She wasn't there—presumably she was swallowed back into Hades at that very instant.

A few of us may even remember that Orpheus was one of the Argonauts who joined Jason on his quest for the Golden Fleece. When the rowdy Greek heroes started fighting among themselves, Orpheus strummed his lyre, calming their ruffled tempers. But there's more to Orpheus than the bereaved romantic whose melodies "calmed the hearts of savage beasts." He was also known in ancient Greece as a mystic and religious reformer whose doctrines reshaped Greek spirituality and profoundly influenced the greatest minds of the ancient Western world.

By the time European written history begins in earnest, Orpheus was already more myth than man. By the fourth century B.C.E., Aristotle had trouble believing the man ever even existed. But if the ancient accounts are true, Orpheus was probably born in Thrace (just northeast of Greece in the area we'd call Bulgaria today) sometime—perhaps *quite* some time—before 700 B.C.E.

The Thracian people were notorious warriors, famous for rushing into battle drunk. Orpheus was not of this mold. Though he was son of the king Oiagros, he took after his mother, whom the texts describe as a muse (an intelligent and cultured woman). While most of his peers were fighting and drinking, he was composing poetry and mastering musical instruments.

In the first century B.C.E., the historian Diodorus Siculus wrote that of poets and musicians, Orpheus was "easily the best of those we remember," that even plants and animals wept at the beauty of his music. The roughneck atmosphere of Thrace must have been a nightmare for the sensitive young man. According to Diodorus he soon made what must have been the most significant decision of his life: to leave his homeland and study in Egypt.

The Greeks stood in awe of Egypt, an ancient culture of immense learning and wealth, renowned for the sublimity of its spiritual tradition. They even recognized that some of their most valued myths were borrowed from the Egyptians, noting that Demeter was the Greek version of Isis and that Athena (after whom the city of Athens was named) was also originally an Egyptian goddess. Egyptian priests were custodians of a legacy of religious and historical knowledge believed to date back tens of thousands of years. Along the banks of the Nile Orpheus would have learned philosophy, ritual, age-old techniques of self-purification, and the mysteries of life after death, a subject of endless fascination for the Egyptians.

When Orpheus reappeared in Thrace, he must have seemed

like a visitor from outer space. More mature now and fantastically charismatic, he brought back philosophy, science, and ethics beyond anything his countrymen could have imagined. Some of them embraced his new doctrine and lifestyle with fierce commitment. Others felt threatened by his teachings, which promised to overthrow their untamed way of life.

## Dionysus: Celebrating Life

To understand the situation Orpheus was facing, you need to know that many Thracians were devotees of Dionysus, god of the raw life force. This expressed itself as lust, intoxication, and uninhibited violence. It was a kind of prehistoric religion of "sex, drugs, and rock and roll," with a Holy Roller twist, as devotees gave themselves up to possession by the god. Dancing and rampaging in the streets, the bacchants (as Dionysus' followers were called) shocked the more conservative element of Greek society, who complained that to invoke Dionysus was to court madness. Even today we watch people who live Dionysian lifestyles—like the wilder of our rock stars—burn out their life force through overindulgence or overdoses. Yet to deny the god, the ancients admitted, also produced insanity. This we still see today too: overly repressed individuals are often neurotic and depressed.

Women were passionate practitioners of this religion. It offered them divine dispensation to throw off the rigid, constricted roles assigned them by Greek society and run wild in the woods, unleashing their frustrations by ripping living animals (and sometimes male relatives) limb from limb, if the legends are true. Eating the raw flesh of a freshly dismembered victim was one way of partaking of Dionysus' life force. If Athena, the goddess of wisdom, was born from Zeus' head, Dionysus was born from his "thigh," a euphemism for *penis*. Emblems of erect phalluses were paraded through the streets in celebration of the primal energy Dionysus represented.

Orpheus—schooled in the far more restrained spirituality of the Egyptian temples—was appalled at the chaos, violence, drunkenness, and sensual overindulgence associated with the rites of Dionysus. According to Greek historians, Orpheus taught the twin laws of karma and reincarnation, and the importance of purifying oneself to obtain freedom from the wheel of rebirth. Calm and temperate, he modeled a nonviolent, contemplative lifestyle that included vegetarianism. Recognizing that it was hopeless to try to suppress the popular religion of his home country, Orpheus worked instead to redirect the bloody Dionysian rites. Traditionally, Thracians ate raw meat and drank gallons of mead during their orgies of communion with their god. Orpheus instructed bacchants to use bread instead of meat and only small quantities of wine during the rites in which they psychically merged with their savior by eating his "body" and drinking his "blood."

## The Meaning in the Myth

Orpheus looked for underlying significance in the timeless myths of Dionysus, a current of hidden knowledge often forgotten in the frenzy of dancing and music at the wine god's festivals. According to legend, Dionysus' mother was one of Zeus' many mortal lovers and certainly one of the most ambitious. In exchange for her love, she demanded that Zeus reveal himself to her in his true form. She literally wanted to see God. Zeus refused at first but when she persisted, he reluctantly granted her wish. The sight of pure divinity annihilated her as completely as the Sun erases the New Moon from the sky. Out of compassion, Zeus rescued the crescent moon–like fetus from her womb and nurtured it in his own body. After the divine child Dionysus was born, the boy-god restored his mother to life, granting her immortality and placing her among the stars.

What does this puzzling story really mean? Yoga students today know that, like Dionysus' mother, all of us carry the potential to become divine beings. Through loving mystical union with God, we can finally achieve a vision of the divine reality, but it will destroy everything we have ever been. It shatters our mortality and gives birth to the living experience of our immortal spirit, the *true* Dionysus. It is this living knowledge that earns the soul a place in heaven.

But the myth continues, and it gets grim. The Titans—antigods of Greek theology—were fiercely jealous of the child god and conspired to kill him. They lured the little boy away from the safety of his father's watchful gaze with a mirror and a set of toys. The boy caught a glimpse of his own beautiful face in the mirror and, completely captivated, failed to notice the monsters creeping up around him. The Titans tore his body to pieces and ate the raw flesh.

The goddess Athena witnessed the crime and rushed to alert Zeus—but it was too late. Zeus avenged his son's gruesome death by hurling his thunderbolt at the Titans, reducing them to ash. This ash is quite important in Greek mythology: the human race was born from it and, at death, returns to it. Meanwhile Athena located Dionysus' still-beating heart—the only part of him the Titans hadn't devoured—and from this organ re-created the boy-god.

What did the original framers of the Dionysus myth mean by these bizarre details? Orpheus had been educated in Egyptian spirituality, centered on a similar story of the death and dismemberment of the Egyptian god Osiris. (Ancient Greek authorities speculated that Osiris and Dionysus represented the same figure.) His interpretation of the story may have gone something like this:

Dionysus is more than raw life force. He is the inner life of the universe itself, the unified consciousness of the cosmos. The Titans—primal energies inherent in matter—seduce consciousness away from itself by revealing to it the extraordinary beauty of nature. Beauty is what spontaneously manifests when spirit "glances" at matter. Matter instantly shapes itself into pleasing forms that distract awareness from its own formless heart.

When consciousness peers into the mirror of matter and sees its own loveliness reflected back, it forgets its real nature. Now it becomes vulnerable to the Titans, who shred the one spirit into a vast number of souls. Nature "swallows" consciousness, and mortality—the union of undying spirit with a perishable body—flickers into existence. The oceanic field of unified consciousness now appears as an infinite number of individual souls caught in physical bodies.

Athena—divine wisdom—is able to restore the lost state of unity. By embracing wisdom, meditating on our innermost heart, our unity with divine being is restored. Dionysus is the ecstasy of cosmic consciousness, not physical intoxication. This state is accessible to those who withdraw from their "titanic" or earthly nature to reclaim their divine heritage.

Orpheus taught that it requires many lifetimes of self-purification to reach this goal. An austere and contemplative life, rooted in respect for all life as an extension of one's own life, is the way to enlightenment.

In *The Masks of God*, Joseph Campbell states the obvious, that Orpheus' teaching is "a system both of thought and practice, exactly paralleling that of Indian asceticism." I'll have much more to say about the connections between Egypt, where Orpheus went to study, and India later in this book.

If the legends are true, Orpheus' life ended tragically, with a horrible, ironic twist. He had founded a brotherhood of initiates, men who devoted their lives to the inner quest for the true Dionysus. Though there were numerous female Orphics in later centuries, Orpheus originally initiated only men and encouraged celibacy as part of their spiritual discipline. Apparently, there was fierce resentment among some of the Thracian women, who were angry that many of their finest men were being seduced away to a reformed religion that seemed to turn its back on the world. In a fit of Dionysian frenzy, the story goes, they attacked Orpheus and ripped his body apart, just as the Titans had torn Dionysus to pieces in the myth.

## "I Am the True Vine"

It is impossible to overestimate the impact of Orpheus' message on the ancient Greeks. Centuries after his death, his teaching still profoundly influenced many of the greatest minds of the European world, from Pythagoras to Plato to Apollonius to Plotinus. Yet ironically, the sage whose tradition he may have influenced most was a first-century rabbi named Jesus.

In the Orphic mysteries Dionysus, the god of wine, says, "I am the vine, and you are my branches," because he is the central stem or universal spirit in which every soul—every "branch" of individual consciousness, you and I—is rooted. Amazingly, in John 15:5, Jesus quotes these very words. Anyone reading this passage in the first few centuries c.e. would instantly recognize that Jesus was pointedly identifying himself with Dionysus—the "All Soul" from which each soul takes its being.

Shortly before his crucifixion, Jesus set about establishing his own mystery religion based in part on the Orphic rites. The sacrament of the Last Supper is patterned not on the Jewish meal at Passover, in which an animal is sacrificed and eaten, but on the Orphic ritual, in which the savior himself is devoured. Jesus explicitly states, "This wine is my blood, this bread is my flesh—take and eat," a ceremony borrowed from the tamer Orphic reenactment of the ancient Dionysian rite. Jesus assumes both Dionysus' traditional roles as "son of God" and "divine bridegroom." Even Dionysus' power of transforming water into wine was reassigned to Jesus.

I had always wondered about early Christian groups, now considered heretical, who saw Holy Communion—a solemn ritual these days—as an opportunity to get drunk, overeat, and have sex. (In 1 Corinthians 11:21, even St. Paul complains about the heavy drinking that occurred during Communion.) Once I understood the connection with Dionysus, the explanation was obvious. Some of the first Christians identified Jesus with Dionysus so literally that they celebrated Communion as a Dionysian orgy!

The connection between Jesus and Orpheus was not lost on early Christians. Scholars have long noted that in Christian catacombs Jesus was portrayed in Thracian clothing holding a lyre: he is actually shown as Orpheus himself! The ancient traditions of depicting Orpheus as "the good shepherd" and as "the fisherman" were borrowed wholesale and transferred directly to Christ. Incidentally, according to the ancient collection of Jewish lore called the Talmud, Jesus, like Orpheus, spent years studying in Egypt. (The Bible itself states that Jesus was taken to Egypt when he was an infant.)

Finally, Jesus, like Orpheus, was said to have returned from the dead. In a number of respects their teachings are strikingly similar: Renounce violence. Live simply. We are all connected to each other like grapes of the same vine, and we are all connected to divine spirit like branches to a bough.

"I am the child of heaven and earth. But my home is in heaven," reads an Orphic grave amulet uncovered by archaeologists. Orpheus returned from Egypt to teach the savage men and women of Europe about dimensions of their inner being few of them had explored. No wonder the Greeks and later the Romans hailed him as one of humanity's greatest saviors.

In the centuries that followed, other Greek sages continued to explore the mysteries of life, from the origin of the cosmos to the nature of physical reality, from the structure of the soul to the qualities of the Supreme Being. They weren't satisfied with the mystery; they wanted an *answer*, a comprehensible truth. Like their peers in India, Egypt, Persia, and Palestine, the Greek sages sought to master both physics and metaphysics. In the next chapter you'll meet the earliest Greek scientist, the most honored of Greece's first generation of sages.

# CHAPTER FOUR

# Helen's Chalice

THALES

FOR THOUSANDS OF YEARS the ancient civilizations of the Near East, India, Egypt, and China fostered sciences amazingly advanced for their time, technologies that astound us even today, and schools of philosophy we still study with excitement. But in Europe, *something went wrong*.

The Greeks themselves acknowledged that the Persians had their Magi, the Babylonians their Chaldeans, the Hindus their yogis, and the Egyptians their priests. Even the seemingly uncivilized Celts had their Druids. But where were the sages, scientists, and historians of prehistoric Greece? Even the dimmest hints of their existence could scarcely be traced. Today we know advanced cultures like the Minoans once flourished in the Mediterranean, but somewhere between 1200 and 800 B.C., southern European civilization collapsed. Scientific knowledge all but vanished. Literacy disappeared.

Scholars debate the cause of this calamity. Was it a prolonged drought that brought southern Europeans to their knees? Warfare? Plague? Could it have been a volcanic eruption, like the famous explosion on the Aegean island Thera, which doomed the Minoans? Was it earthquakes and tsunamis? My guess is that it must have taken some combination of these factors to erase so much of the wisdom of Europe's earlier generations.

The Greeks clung to the songs of Homer and Hesiod, composed perhaps about 800 B.C., like children to their mother's skirt, an orphaned culture desperately trying to remember its past. Their lineages of priests and bards had ceased to exist, and with them the knowledge that this caste preserved in all other Indo-European societies: history, star lore, ritual magic, meditation techniques. At many sites only untrained volunteers were left to take turns running the temples of Greece.

The Greeks needed to resurrect themselves. They would either have to re-create their wisdom tradition or live out their lives in a wasteland of ignorance and anarchy.

## The Star Gazer

By 600 B.C. the Greeks were starting over from scratch, taking their cues from teachers who had studied in countries unaffected by the cataclysm that shook southern Europe. Foremost of these was Thales of Miletus.

At this time the Oracle at Delphi was the spiritual center of the Greek world. Here pilgrims could consult directly with the god Apollo, who spoke to them through the seeress at his temple there. One day she received two especially agitated delegations. One was from Miletus, a town near the southern tip of eastern Turkey. The other was from the island of Cos. They were about to go to war—unless the Oracle could resolve their dispute.

It turned out a fisherman from Cos had sold a basketful of fish to merchants from Miletus. Sorting though the fish, the Miletians discovered a stunning golden chalice. This was a priceless find; they were sure it must be the legendary drinking bowl Helen had cast into the sea on her voyage home from Troy. Helen was the woman whose beauty had "launched a thousand ships" sent to bring her back to her husband, the famous events Homer chronicled in the *Iliad*. The Miletians could scarcely believe their luck that the Cosians hadn't noticed the chalice in their fishing net.

Now the men of Cos were up in arms, insisting they had sold only the fish, not the bowl, and should have the bowl back. The men of Miletus insisted they had paid for the contents of the basket, whatever was in it. Who was right?

The seeress went into a trance and answered, "The bowl does not belong to the men of Cos. Nor does it belong to the men of Miletus. It belongs to the wisest man in Greece."

Apollo had spoken. There was nothing to do but turn the bowl over to its rightful owner. The two delegations agreed this could be none other than Thales.

Why would they have chosen Thales above all other men and women for this distinction? Thales is the first Greek known to correctly predict eclipses, use geometry, define the summer and winter solstices, and set up a calendar of 365 days—all skills he would have learned in Egypt. To his uneducated countrymen in the early sixth century B.C.E., these abilities must have seemed nearly miraculous.

Though Thales had traveled to Egypt to learn from the priests and astronomers there, he spent most of his life in Miletus. There he adamantly resisted the pressure to conform to the norms of Greek life. When his mother first tried to push him into marriage, he objected, saying he was too young. Years later when she badgered him again, he complained he was too old. He wasn't interested in wasting his genius on some boring job, either. Instead he used his keen understanding of nature to foresee an exceptional growing season for olives. He rented all the oil presses in the area and made himself a quick fortune he was able to live off the rest of his life.

The profoundest of advice, "Know thyself," emblazoned

over the portal at the temple of Delphi, is attributed to Thales. Yet this wisest of men may also have been the original prototype of the absent-minded professor. In one particularly famous account, Thales went out at night to observe the stars, astronomy being among his greatest interests, and fell into a ditch. The elderly woman who heard him calling for help couldn't resist offering some advice of her own as she pulled him out. "How can you expect to know the secrets of heaven, Thales, when you don't know what's in front of your own two feet?"

Another report mentions a man who was being hauled into divorce court after being discovered having an affair. He asked Thales if it was okay to deny the charge, even though he would be under oath. Thales wryly observed, "Well, my dear boy, perjury is no worse than adultery." It's nice to know that, for all his intellect, the man had a sense of humor.

Thales was deeply spiritual; the concept that a person couldn't be both religious and scientific at the same time had not yet been invented in the West. He taught that all of nature is alive and filled with divinity. Pressed on the question of life after death, he confidently affirmed the immortality of the soul.

When asked if he thought men could hide their evil deeds from the gods, he responded, "No. Nor evil thoughts, either." His ethics were straightforward. He claimed the best moral standard was to "avoid doing the things you criticize other people for doing." A happy life, he said, was assured to those who "maintain a healthy body, a relaxed disposition, and an active mind."

There's still more to Thales' résumé. He was also a skilled engineer and statesman. He diverted the flow of the river Halys for King Croesus, and astutely urged his fellow citizens to unite in a confederation against the Persians, who all too soon would be on the attack. (Unfortunately for the Greeks, they ignored his advice.)

At a time when most Greeks were just beginning to awaken from their Dark Age, Thales was listed first among their sages.

## The Golden Bowl

These days Thales is primarily remembered as the ancient Greek who was supposedly so naive he thought the world was produced from water. (In the first few verses of the Bible, we are told that God "brooded over the face of the waters." The concept of cosmic waters from which all life emerged was an age-old doctrine in Egypt, the Near East, and India.) But this largely forgotten thinker and scientist made a huge contribution to the development of our civilization. He helped inaugurate an era scholars today call "the Greek miracle," a period that saw squabbling colonies struggling for survival around the Aegean Sea transform themselves into one of the liveliest and most influential cultures in human history.

When the Oracle at Delphi suggested that the Greeks award the golden bowl to the most brilliant man among them, they presented it to Thales. He was embarrassed by the honor and tried to pass the prize along to other highly regarded Greeks. Out of respect, each one of them returned the chalice to him. Finally he sent it back to Apollo's temple at Delphi with the message, "Apollo is the wisest of all."

Thales was the earliest of a remarkable group of thinkers scholars today call "the pre-Socratics." These were the most influential sages of the Western world before Socrates and his famous disciple, Plato. We know frustratingly little about these men—and it doesn't help that the information we do have is fragmentary and often contradictory. But we do know a fair bit more about Thales' most famous pupil, one of the greatest spiritual masters in the history of Western civilization. You'll meet him next.

# CHAPTER FIVE

# The Spiritual Colony

## PYTHAGORAS

ONE OF THE MOST INFLUENTIAL spiritual communities in Europe was located along the southeastern edge of the boot of Italy. There were about six hundred members, some of whom lived on the ashram premises and the rest of whom commuted in from outlying areas. It wasn't unusual for as many as two thousand people to show up for specially scheduled programs.

In many respects it was a typical ashram. The devotees were vegetarians, they didn't drink or take drugs, they dressed in white, they got up before sunrise to do stretching exercises and sit for meditation. They practiced long periods of silence, and sex outside marriage was considered inappropriate—even for the famously risqué Italians!

Body work, particularly massage, was popular there, and diet was a major focus. The menu was built around fresh vegetables (raw or lightly cooked), herbs, and grains. Students wore weights around their wrists during their daily exercise routines to enhance their workouts.

The community was particularly known for its music therapy program. Therapists there claimed to have achieved success in treating certain diseases, particularly some types of mental illness, with soothing music.

The founder was a brilliant, charismatic teacher who was regarded with a certain amount of suspicion by local authorities. His devotees believed he knew their past lives and could lead them to enlightenment.

If you'd like to visit the community, you can fly into Naples, rent a car, and drive southeast to Croton. However, once you reach the south coast, you'll have trouble locating it, because the community burned down twenty-five hundred years ago.

## Spiritual History

As is so often the case in spiritual history, our story begins before the beginning. In the distant recesses of prehistory, a devotee named Aethalides propitiated Hermes, the wisdom god of the Greeks and Egyptians, hoping to secure the greatest boon a human being can achieve. At last Hermes materialized. "I'm delighted by your worship. Now tell me, what is it you want?"

"Immortality," Aethalides answered squarely.

Hermes rolled his eyes. "Son, there's no way I can give you what I myself don't possess. At the end of the world cycle, even we gods pass away. You'll have to ask for something else."

Aethalides thought carefully. If he couldn't live forever, perhaps he could have the next best thing. "When they're reborn, most people forget their previous lives. They have to start over from scratch, rebuilding their personalities on the basis of a few talents and tendencies carried over from other births. Hermes, let me always remember who I am. In life, in the after-death state, and in all my lives to come, I don't want to lose my identity. Grant me the boon of uninterrupted awareness across all my incarnations."

Now Hermes was grinning broadly. Most humans asked him for psychic powers or the ability to change cheap metals into gold. What a pleasure to finally find a devotee with the intelligence to ask for something of real value! Hermes raised his hand in blessing, and Aethalides got his wish.

Fast-forward across the centuries to about 570 B.C.E. The gem dealer Mnesarchus was visiting the Oracle of Apollo at Delphi, asking if he'd make a good profit on his latest business venture. "Yes," murmured the Pythoness, the most famous seeress in the ancient European world, as she tottered on top of her three-legged stool, inhaling psychoactive fumes of ethylene that waft mysteriously from a crevice in the temple floor. In remote antiquity, the priestess here had served a serpent deity, but the god Apollo had killed the snake and established his own worship at this sacred site. Yet even now the chief priestess here was called the Pythoness, in honor of the great snake.

"But I have better news than that to tell you," the seeress continued. "Your wife is pregnant. Cherish the special soul who's coming to your family. He'll be the greatest man of his generation, a benefactor of humanity whose name will be remembered forever."

Mnesarchus rushed back to Sidon in Phoenicia (about a hundred miles north of Bethlehem) and verified that indeed his wife was expecting a child. There was some question about exactly when she'd conceived—after all, Mnesarchus had been traveling on business for some time—which in later years would ignite speculation that the child's real father had been none other than the god Apollo himself.

Mnesarchus' son was born some months later. From the beginning there was something unusual about him. Maybe it was the way that, even as an infant, he stared you right in the eye, as if he were already fully self-aware, as if he already knew himself and you too. Mnesarchus named his son after the Pythoness who had foretold his destiny: he called the boy Pythagoras. Later the boy would claim his name had once been Aethalides, that he had

been a devotee of Hermes, and that he vividly remembered everything he'd learned in all his previous incarnations.

Mnesarchus moved his family back to Samos, his home island
on the east coast of the Aegean Sea. Bearing the words of the
prophetess in mind, he spared no expense in educating his son.
Pythagoras studied with the renowned physicist Anaximander,
and with Thales of Miletus, who is still remembered as "the father
of science" in our own era. Thales was so impressed by the young
man's inherent genius that he insisted, "You must go to Egypt
and learn from the masters who taught me. If you study with the
priests at Memphis, you'll become the wisest of the Greeks."

From Thales, Pythagoras learned the disciplines he would
need to win the respect of the great gurus of Egypt. He became a
vegetarian, gave up alcohol (for the rest of his life he would drink
only water), and severely limited the amount of time he devoted
to sleep. He decided to sail to Egypt by way of his boyhood home
in Syria in order to seek initiation in the Phoenician mysteries.
Then he would approach the Egyptian masters who, it was said,
had originally instructed the Phoenician hierophants long ago.

Pythagoras' Syrian teachers sent him to Mount Carmel, where
he spent months in solitary meditation. Mount Carmel, pocked
with innumerable caves, had been a meditation retreat from remote times. Gnostic masters called the Mandeans claimed that the
great sages of the Semitic traditions flew to Mount Carmel in their
subtle bodies for regular conferences.

From Phoenicia Pythagoras sailed to Egypt, where he studied for twenty-two years. Iamblichus, a Syrian master of the third
century C.E., reported, "Pythagoras visited the important temples
in Egypt, where he won the admiration of the priests for his
diligent studies and detailed research into their tradition. There
was no sage he did not seek out, nor any Egyptian school he neglected. If he thought he could learn from someone, he set out to

find them. He passed twenty-two years in the study of astronomy and astrology, geometry, and the spiritual mysteries."

Pythagoras' next stop was Babylon. From the Magi he learned music, mathematics, and other Chaldean sciences. According to the early Christian writer Clement of Alexandria, Pythagoras also studied with the brahmins of India. It's unlikely he made it all the way to India itself, but he probably studied with Hindu teachers known to have immigrated to Babylon. After twelve years in Persia, now in the fifty-sixth year of his life, Pythagoras headed home to Greece, hoping to share the treasure trove of wisdom he'd accumulated during his pilgrimages.

## The Spiritual Community

Pythagoras tried at first to found his ashram, rooted in the teachings of Egypt and the East, on the island of Samos. When he arrived he found a group of fishermen hauling in nets full of fish. "If I tell you exactly how many fish you've caught between you, will you do as I suggest?" he asked. Since there was no way he could know the right number of fish, they laughingly agreed. But when they did the count, it turned out Pythagoras had been correct. He then asked them to return the fish to the sea. Remarkably, the fish had survived their ordeal and leapt gratefully back into the water. Pythagoras then paid the fishermen the amount they had lost on the day's catch and went on his way. The fishermen quickly spread the story of the remarkable visitor throughout the small Greek island.

Pythagoras spent most of his time in Samos meditating in a cave. Occasionally he would emerge to teach the Greeks astonishing things such as the mathematics of the celestial spheres, how to calculate eclipses, and the motions of the planets. The movements and patterns of the entire universe were based on arithmetical principles and geometric forms, he said. For Pythagoras science meant understanding the underlying principles of the cosmos. In fact, he was the first to use the word *cosmos,* which meant "an ordered universe." (A universe without order was called "chaos.") He was also the first person known to call himself a "philosopher," which meant "lover of wisdom."

However, the Greeks at Samos simply wanted to see more miracles. They weren't interested in actually doing the spiritual disciplines Pythagoras was eager to teach. Finally he moved to southern Italy, where he found better-quality students. A large group of devotees quickly gathered around him, helping him build the famous spiritual colony at Croton. Soon the size of the audience that regularly showed up to hear his lectures became so huge, the ancients compared the auditorium where he taught to a small city.

The Pythagorean community became famous for its harmonious workings: relationships were built on unshakable friendship, mutual respect, and forgiveness. Members shared their goods in common. If members decided to leave the group, however, they were allowed to take back the items they had brought with them.

Though he had practiced asceticism most of his life, the master didn't feel strict celibacy was a prerequisite for spiritual life. He eventually married and raised several children. We know he believed in strong families and considered it a tragedy when a child came from a broken home.

Women were honored in Pythagoras' community. We are told that one of Pythagoras' gurus was the priestess Themistoklea of Delphi, who taught ethics. Pythagoras encouraged women to study philosophy and cosmology and to assume roles of spiritual leadership. Centuries later, when Iamblichus listed the most illustrious Pythagoreans, he included seventeen women.

Pythagoras married Theano of Croton, a woman with a reputation for exceptional wisdom and integrity in her own right. She had been raised in the Orphic tradition, and along with her husband was a strong believer in reincarnation. "If the soul wasn't immortal," she said, "life would be a feast for evildoers." This universe returns to equilibrium, so a person who lives honorably invariably invokes a positive response from the cosmos, whether it comes in this life or the next. Those who commit evil deeds, she taught, would also reap the consequences of their behavior, possibly even being reborn in subhuman form.

Theano would not have been impressed by our modern society's preoccupation with sexuality. Devoting too much time to romance, she taught, was "the natural inclination of an empty soul." Her daughters Arignote and Myia would go on to become leaders in their community.

Today Pythagoras' name is often linked with numerology. Number mysticism was unquestionably part of his contemplative path. He taught his disciples to meditate on numbers, ratios, geometric forms, and even musical chords in order to appreciate the order and structure of the natural world. Harmonious patterns, reverberating from the One, lay at the root of all phenomena, he said.

Theano complained that people misunderstood her husband as claiming that the universe is created from numbers. "He didn't say things come *from* numbers," she wrote, "but *in accordance with* number. Number is a principle, not a material entity. Number creates order and sequence. Because formulas and ratios underlie the universe, the world is ordered rather than chaotic." This Pythagorean vision of the mathematical principles lying behind nature would become the foundation of Western science.

## Pythagorean Precepts

Pythagoras was famous for his enigmatic sayings. These were short statements that sounded cryptic or even silly. At his lectures Pythagoras would "unpack" their hidden meanings. For example:

"Don't poke a fire with a sword." This was an admonition not to make someone who's upset with you even more irritated by responding with anger.

"Keep your bags packed." Death can come at any time. Be prepared.

"When you reach the border, don't look back." At the time of death, release the past.

"Don't leave your post without the order of your commanding officer." Do not commit suicide.

"When you worship, sit down." Don't rush through your spiritual practices.

"Don't write in the snow." Don't waste your time teaching people who don't appreciate the value of what you have to offer.

Words of advice from Pythagoras and his chief disciples were preserved by many ancient authors such as Sextus, Iamblichus, and Stobaeus:

"People bring their problems on themselves. Failing to see the good around them, they entangle themselves in self-created difficulties."

"People run in every direction meeting sorrow after sorrow. Why? Because they're disconnected from themselves."

"First of all, respect yourself."

"Think before you act."

"Desire to do good for your enemies."

"Don't ask God to give you anything you can lose."

"Don't value anything anyone can take away from you."

"Don't bother packing things you won't need on your journey to the next world."

"If you rule over others, bear in mind that God rules over you."

"We don't have the power to live forever, but we do have the power to live ethically."

"Fear of death exists only in those who are ignorant of their own souls."

"If you want to know your Maker, know yourself."

"Don't be so eager to help a man lay down his burden. This could make him lazy. Instead help him *carry* his burden."

"Unless you have something to say more pleasing than silence, don't break the silence."

"For the greedy, life is like a funeral banquet. They're surrounded by delicious food, but even so they're not happy."

"Drunkenness is meditation on insanity."

"The first step is half the journey."

"Be guided by discriminating wisdom, the highest and best part of you. If you do this, when you die you will not die, but be transformed into something divine."

## Destroying the Dream

Pythagoras had a dramatically transformative effect on the lives of his students, who enthusiastically embraced self-discipline, high ethical standards, and contemplation. "He doesn't teach," they reported, "he cures souls."

Some members of nearby cities were so impressed by the wisdom and virtue of the community that they invited Pythagoras and his chief disciples to arbitrate their disputes. This was the beginning of the end. Inevitably the Pythagoreans' involvement in politics was seen as meddling, and enemies began to plot revenge. On one of the darkest days in ancient European history, a group of thugs attacked the ashram, burning its facilities and killing everyone they could find. An early experiment in what we today would call a yogic lifestyle came to a shattering end.

Some say Pythagoras himself survived the fire, but if that's true, we hear no more of him. His entire life he'd worked to call forth the best in humanity. That final horrible day he'd seen humanity at its worst. It must have broken his heart.

Ironically, today Pythagoras is remembered for a mathematical axiom he didn't invent. Scholars have shown that the so-called Pythagorean theorem was already known much earlier in India and Egypt. We've forgotten that in his own time Pythagoras was best known as a spiritual master, a guru of the highest caliber whose teachings would survive over the next few centuries to profoundly influence the greatest minds of ancient Western civilization—as you'll soon see.

CHAPTER SIX

# The Road to Reality

PARMENIDES

ONE OF THE MOST INFLUENTIAL philosophers of antiquity was
Parmenides of Elea. Born in southwestern Italy sometime around
515 B.C.E., he dominated Western thought for centuries.

We are told that Parmenides was born into a wealthy, prominent Greek family. He was good-looking and carried himself
with dignity, qualities that helped him succeed in politics; his
work in the Eleatic legislature was highly praised. Yet this powerful, successful man was drawn to spirituality and studied with
several remarkable spiritual teachers.

One was Xenophanes of Colophon, who taught that there
were not many gods but one, and that this single Supreme Being
was a vast and eternal mind. (Xenophanes also pointed out that
you could find fossils of sea creatures on mountaintops, proof
that the mountains had once been under water. Xenophanes was
by no means the first person to notice this. Similar discoveries
thousands of years earlier probably gave rise to the worldwide
myth of the Great Flood.) It was Parmenides' encounter with a
Pythagorean named Ameinias, however, that turned him to a life
of contemplation.

Parmenides wrote only one short book—a long poem, really

—yet his words were so compelling they earned him centuries of fame. He described a mythical journey that led him into the presence of a majestic goddess. The mares pulling his chariot were guided by two maidens he called "Daughters of the Sun." Between the two large wheels on either side of the chariot, Parmenides took pains to note, the axle made a "shrill sound like a pipe." Eventually, he came to the twin Gates of Day and Night, which a guardian named Dike allowed him to pass through. Finally he met the Goddess of Truth herself, who welcomed him warmly and promised to reveal the supreme secret of the universe and to expose the illusions about the nature of the world that typically mislead mortal men.

## The Inner Journey

Unfortunately, only fragments of this poem have survived. Modern scholars have wrestled with these bits and pieces in an effort to pin down the revelation that so impressed Parmenides' many ancient admirers—or jarred his detractors. Those of us trained in meditative traditions (which could well be similar to those taught by Parmenides' Pythagorean teacher), may offer insights into Parmenides' journey that nonmeditators lack.

The chariot our pilgrim rides is his own body. The "straining mares" who try to pull it one way, then another, are the five senses. Plato later repeats this analogy, but it appears much earlier in the scriptures of India.

The Daughters of the Sun who lead the chariot forward represent the pilgrim's eyes, while the two large wheels on the side of the vehicle are his ears. As for the "shrill sound like a pipe" in between the wheels, from time immemorial meditators have used subtle sounds within the brain and inner ear as a point of focus. Pythagoras himself had spoken of "the music of the spheres," sounds most of us don't hear because we're so used to them. He explained that we've been immersed in these subtle sounds from birth and no longer notice unless we pay close attention. This Pythagorean music must surely be the inner sounds yogis associate with the seven planets externally and the seven chakras (centers of consciousness in the subtle body) internally. Here Parmenides refers specifically to the "shrill sound" we meditators instantly notice when we shift our full awareness to the center of our brain.

The Gates of Day and Night our pilgrim needs to open in order to gain access to the Goddess must be the two nostrils. In India, in fact, they're specifically called the paths of the Sun and Moon. Most of the time air flows through one or the other of our nostrils predominantly. Traditionally trained meditators focus on the nasal septum between the nostrils, which causes air to flow equally on both sides of the nose, slowly, softly, and smoothly. Surprisingly this has a dramatic effect on consciousness, producing a tremendous sense of clarity and tranquility. When these two gates opened for Parmenides, he was psychologically and physiologically prepared for a divine vision.

Interestingly, Parmenides said that it was the goddess Dike who controlled the entrance to this higher state of consciousness. Dike, whose name is usually translated as "justice," represents what yoga students today would call karma. Only souls who are adequately pure and self-disciplined have ready access to higher states. It is Dike who cleared the way for a meeting with an even greater goddess, the Goddess of Truth.

Later Greeks would name the mysterious Goddess of Truth Parmenides encounters on his meditative journey Hypsipyle, which means "the highest gate." It appears that Parmenides was holding his awareness at the crown chakra or highest focus point at the top of the brain when he had his remarkable vision. Hypsipyle represents the force the yogics call *guru shakti*, the intelligence at the heart of the universe that guides and illuminates devotees who find their way into her presence.

The Goddess teaches Parmenides to distinguish between eternal, unchanging reality and the unstable world of the senses, between the absolute and the relative. Pure existence is continuous *being*, indivisible, without beginning or end, never altered in any way, a perfect unity, she explains. In it there is no creation or destruction, no motion of any kind, simply being itself. If this sounds abstract, it's because there isn't really any way to describe it—you can't compare it with anything else. However, with mental focus any of us can experience this extraordinary state directly, just as Parmenides did.

Though there's nothing "in" it, pure being isn't empty. It's *not* "nothing." All you can accurately say is "it is." In fact, the Goddess doesn't even use the word *it*, just *is*. You can't even say it's eternal, using words like *was* or *will be*, because time doesn't exist for it. It just—is.

This is probably the pure being the Bible refers to when God says simply, "I am what I am" (Exodus 3:14) because no other word than simply *am* can possibly describe him. In James 1:17 the Bible is even more explicit, referring to "the Father of Light in whom there is no change or even the shadow of change." How can this Lord of Light be known? "Be still and know that I am God" (Psalms 46:10), the Bible advises. Only profound stillness, like the meditative stillness Parmenides enters on his inner journey, can lead us to the highest portal.

Similarly, at the temple of Delphi a cryptic message inscribed on the wall states simply, "Thou art." It refers to the greatest of all mysteries, pure being beyond words and images.

Advanced meditators experience precisely this reality in a state yogis call *nirvikalpa samadhi*. When a saint manages to integrate this awareness fully into her life, so that she feels this pure beingness, whether she's sitting in meditation, working, or even sleeping, it's called *sahaja samadhi*.

## Facing Reality

Needless to say, this reality existing outside time, space, and causation isn't exactly what most of us experience most of the time. Eating breakfast, driving to work, watching television, we move through a world that's full of constantly changing colors and sounds.

The Goddess warns that the universe we normally perceive is a sort of illusion. What truly exists doesn't come and go like a television program, a job, or a failed marriage. Something that's *really* real has no beginning or end, it just is. The Goddess encourages Parmenides to think this through carefully. Even as his five senses present him with an evolving world full of different objects, he must use his intellect to cut through it to the deeper truth behind it, the unchanging awareness that contains it all.

Parmenides' Goddess points out that our focus on duality—light and dark, hot and cold, past and present—shifts our awareness away from the timeless, unitary whole of pure being. Individual objects and the sequence of time—limits imposed by number—appear. Boundaries are imposed on infinity, and we mistakenly believe "I end here and you start there" rather than "we are all absolutely One."

Is this "is-ness" just some philosophical abstraction? No. Just like the yogis of India, Parmenides says is-ness is *consciousness*. And everything that exists, even rocks and stones, participates in this living awareness.

Don't misunderstand him, though; Parmenides does *not* deny the practical reality of the day-to-day world. For all his apparent otherworldliness, Parmenides was a down-to-earth man. Though recognized as one of ancient Greece's greatest thinkers, he was also honored as a scientist and healer. In an inscription discovered at an archaeological site at Elea, Parmenides is hailed as "a natural philosopher and physician." "Natural philosopher" meant something like "theoretical physicist" does today. He was a doctor too. A philosopher with his head in the clouds doesn't usually treat patients.

As a scientist, Parmenides taught that the Earth is a sphere, that the Sun and Moon are part of the Milky Way, and that stars are compressed masses of fire. He was interested in biology too, teaching, for example, that homosexuality is created in an embryo at the moment of conception, as some geneticists today suspect. (Ancient Greece was one of the most pro-gay cultures in history.) However, while the senses offer us a world filled with diversity that as embodied beings we have to deal with, the enlightened mind sees through it to the unchanging unity that encompasses it.

But if everything we experience is ultimately One, why do we experience a universe filled with seemingly separate things? The ultimate cause behind all these appearances is the Great Goddess herself, Parmenides wrote. She dwells "in the midst of all things" and "sends souls from the invisible realms into the visible world, and calls them back again." She created the gods, the first of whom was Eros, "desire." The universe appears through the mixture and separation of qualities that are light, bright, and intelligent with ones that are heavy, dark, and inert. It's remarkable how close this explanation comes to the ancient Indian notion that the manifestation of the universe is really the interplay of three qualities: *rajas* (motion), *sattva* (which is light, bright, intelligent), and *tamas* (which is heavy, dark, and inert).

## Lead Us from the Unreal

As some of you readers familiar with Eastern traditions may already be thinking, it wouldn't be entirely inappropriate to call

Parmenides "the Shankaracharya of Greece." Indeed if the histories preserved in the oldest Advaita Vedanta monasteries of India are accurate, Parmenides and Shankaracharya lived at about the same time. There are some eerie parallels between the teachings of these two legendary masters.

Shankara (the title *acharya* means "honored teacher") was a devotee of the goddess Lalita, whose worship he established in the four corners of India. Lalita projected the gods out of herself, the first of whom was Kama, "desire." (Very ancient myths from both India and Greece claim the world can't be created until "desire" for experience first appears.) Lalita is pure consciousness itself, seen as a living, dynamic, intelligent force.

Shankara taught that the only reality is Brahman, pure conscious being. It is beyond time, space, and causation, completely pure, perfect, and unchanging. We misperceive the universe as multifaceted, while in reality it is completely unitary. The mental process involved in this misunderstanding is called *maya*. *Maya* literally means "measuring the immeasurable." Because of the way our mind and senses process information, we see separation and suffering where there is only pure self-existence. Shankara preached the doctrine of *satkaryavad,* meaning that nothing new or different from the Supreme Reality can ever be produced. Everything we experience is simply a mental transformation of the one reality, and nothing more.

If this sounds far-fetched, try thinking of the vivid events you experience in a dream. Real as they seem, the people and objects there are nothing other than your own mental figments, existing nowhere but in the field of your own consciousness. The waking world is just another level of maya, of the dream, according to Shankara. The men and women we call enlightened are those who have awakened to the complete, seamless unity of reality.

How do you wake up? Exactly as did Parmenides, Shankara

recommended *jnana* yoga, the path of the intellect. You must exert the full force of your intelligence to reason your way through maya and finally, in the depths of meditation, actually experience the living truth itself. Though they lived on different continents, Parmenides and Shankara seem to have been operating on exactly the same wavelength.

One of the oldest prayers in India begins *Asatoma sad gamaya,* "From the unreal, lead us to reality." After Parmenides, every Greek thinker would have to think very carefully about what was "really real." And some of them, like the formidable sage you'll meet next, had very different views.

# CHAPTER SEVEN

# The Private Investigator

## HERACLITUS

"YOU CAN NEVER STEP in the same river twice."
"The only thing that never changes is change."
"The road up is the road down."
"If you don't expect the unexpected, you won't find it."
"A man's character is his fate."

We still use these phrases today, unaware that they originated twenty-five hundred years ago. They were first spoken by a Greek sage named Heraclitus, a contemporary of Parmenides who lived in Ephesus, a city on the coast of western Turkey, not far north of Miletus, where we found Thales a century earlier.

Heraclitus was not a "nice" guy. Unabashedly arrogant, he rarely had anything good to say about anyone, even Homer, the poet genius of Greek civilization. Homer was mistaken to include a prayer for peace in the *Iliad*, according to Heraclitus, because conflict is the very essence of reality. "War is king," he flatly declared. Even authors writing about him centuries later couldn't conceal their malice. Clearly, this was a man with a talent for making enemies.

Like Parmenides, Heraclitus became famous because of the only book he ever wrote. There was a serious problem with the book, though: no one could understand it. This gained the curmudgeonly philosopher the unflattering epithet "Heraclitus the Obscure." It was said that Darius, king of Persia, was so impressed with the book—which *seemed* profound—that he asked Heraclitus to come to his court and explain it to him. Heraclitus had no more respect for Darius than he did for anyone else and firmly declined.

Needless to say, scholars today are in a poor position to explain what Heraclitus was talking about when the best minds of his own day weren't completely sure. It doesn't help that not many passages from the book have survived. But this much we can say: Heraclitus saw a universe on fire. "The cosmos was never created, but always was and always will be a living fire, kindled and extinguished in cycles of specific length," he wrote. Physical elements precipitated out of this everlasting fire. In a sense, physicists today who claim matter condensed out of the superenergetic blast of a Big Bang are echoing Heraclitus.

While Parmenides focused on the unchanging stability he sensed behind the changing world of the senses, Heraclitus emphasized conflict and instability. Everything is always in flux, like a river or a flame. A proper understanding of the role of conflict is central to wisdom. Everything in the universe is at odds with everything else; if this weren't the case, the universe couldn't exist! The push and pull of natural forces create the changing stream of events that *are* reality. Without the interplay of opposites, there would be only stasis, death. Strife is life. "War is king."

Heraclitus pointed out that although the cosmos is in constant commotion, it's not chaotic. "That which tears things apart brings them together." You can't have a melody without different notes. You can't perpetuate human life without both female and male. Contrasting elements contending against each other create a greater harmony.

There is a *logos*, a "plan" or "design" that moves the universe. "A vast, unitary wisdom controls all things through all things," Heraclitus wrote. "In all things lies unity; in unity lie all things." Importantly, for Heraclitus "day and night, summer and winter, peace and war" are *both* God. He believed that where ordinary people see good and evil, God sees balance.

One of the most fascinating components of Heraclitus' teaching was his doctrine of the cycles of time. According to ancient authorities, Heraclitus taught that the universe passes in and out of existence, like a fire being kindled, extinguished, and rekindled. This occurs endlessly over the limitless expanses of eternity. The concept that we are all controlled by fate, ruled by the inexorable cycles of time—a very influential idea throughout Greek history—was especially championed by Heraclitus' spiritual heirs, a lineage of spiritual practitioners called the Stoics.

Heraclitus wrote, "The thunderbolt steers all things." For the sages of the Indo-European tradition, from India to Ireland, the thunderbolt represented the spinning double axis of the solstices and equinoxes, the wheel of time. From the moment the world flares back into existence from the universal fire until its ashes blow away at the end of the cycle, rising and falling, winning and losing, life and death are inevitable, and each leads to the other. "The beginning and the end are the same," Heraclitus said.

If this is the case, how then should humans live? We should "think clearly, speak honestly, act wisely, and deepen our awareness," the master admonished.

Heraclitus attacked the religion of his day, especially the animal sacrifices still widely practiced in his time. "They uselessly try to purify themselves with blood when in fact they're only defiling themselves. It's like a man trying to wash himself with mud!" What we really need to cleanse ourselves of is our sense of self-importance. "It's more important to extinguish egotism than a house on fire."

"It's not helpful for people to get everything they want," Heraclitus also said. "No one appreciates health till they're sick, food till they're hungry, or rest till they're exhausted."

While other thinkers explored the secrets of the physical world, Heraclitus focused on a more central mystery. "I investigate myself." Hidden in the deepest recesses of the spirit are the greatest truths. This inner quest is endless. "You'll never find the limits of the soul, no matter how many roads you travel." But inquiring into the nature of our innermost self is exactly what we *must* do. "Self-knowledge is every person's birthright."

While Parmenides and Heraclitus had very different points of emphasis, on one important issue they agreed. Behind all the phenomena of nature lies an infinitely vast intelligence. "If you throw spices in a fire, people say it smells sweet or pungent or acrid. But really there is only fire," Heraclitus wrote. "Our senses reveal many things, but really there is only God."

While Thales was deeply influenced by the Egyptians who, like him, taught that the world arose from water, Heraclitus was inspired by the Persians. Fire was the primary symbol of their religion; for Heraclitus it was the primal metaphor for reality itself. For Persians the conflict between two opposing cosmic forces, Ahura Mazda and Ahriman (God and Satan, so to speak), was central. Heraclitus was also preoccupied with the tension between opposites. The Persians were eminent students of the cycles of time, governed by Zurvan, their god of time (called Maha Kala or Kali by the Persians' Indian neighbors). And Persia was famous for its astrologers, called Magi, who helped people understand the vagaries of fate. The Persians controlled Heraclitus' home city of Ephesus, so it should surprise no one that he was influenced by their worldview.

## The Mound of Manure

Only a few stories about Heraclitus' life have survived, and it's not always clear whether they're true. In one tale he sat in front of the famous temple of Artemis playing dice with a group of children. When several Ephesian statesmen expressed their shock to find him wasting his time this way, he snapped, "Why are you so surprised, you asses? I'm better off here with these stupid kids than with you and your politics!" His sharp tongue was legendary.

Ancient historians report that Heraclitus eventually wandered off into the mountains to be alone, surviving on whatever wild grains he could find. The Greeks considered this yet another sign of his antisocial nature. Today we might wonder if his motivation was more like that of the Indian yogis, if he adopted an isolated, ascetic lifestyle in order to "investigate himself" full-time.

A particularly ungenerous account of Heraclitus' death claims that he suffered from edema (water retention, a possible sign of congestive heart failure). He lay down on the ground and asked some children to cover him with cow dung, assuming that as the dung dried it would leech the excess fluid out of his body. But the children ran away, and the dung hardened as it dried until he couldn't move. Finally, a pack of dogs showed up and made a meal of him.

Modern scholars have noted that it was a Persian practice to leave dead bodies to be eaten by wild animals. (Until a few decades ago, this method of disposing of corpses was still practiced in Tibet.) The truth may be that Heraclitus was simply given a Persian-style funeral but that later Greek writers couldn't pass up one last chance to make fun of the hot-tempered master.

Heraclitus, the ancients agreed, was "a man of riddles." "What did you think of his book?" a disciple asked Socrates—the most famous Greek philosopher of all—a century later. "The part of it I could understand was pretty good," Socrates answered. "And what I didn't understand seemed like it was probably good too. But you have to be a diver to get to the bottom of it!"

## The Eternal Fire

It's unlikely that Heraclitus invented his vision of the universe as unending and uncreated, cycling in and out of manifestation through all eternity. Similar views were expressed in the many Puranas ("Ancient Chronicles") of India. The Stoics who came after him emphasized the need to make peace with the logos, or design of nature, and to do one's duty calmly and ethically.

If Parmenides reminds us of aspects of the yoga tradition that emphasize Shiva, or pure being, Heraclitus' thinking has resonances with the parts of the tradition that emphasize Shakti, or pure becoming. His primeval fire, which both creates and consumes the universe, is similar to Shakti, consciousness as energy or dynamic power. In India time itself is conceived as the goddess Kali, who wields terrifying weapons in some of her hands yet makes gestures of reassurance with others. In Kali both the frightening and benign aspects of nature are perfectly reconciled, war and peace harmonized in a larger whole that simply is what it is. She gives life but ends it also. She provides food and good health but also sends drought and disease. Kali's devotees in India don't overidealize the Goddess. They see her as she is and accept her paradoxical nature.

Heraclitus too had the courage to look eternity in the eye and speak the truth he saw. This won him no friends. But in his declining years, living yogi-like alone in the hills, perhaps this spiritual warrior found some measure of peace as he wandered the endless roads of the soul.

# CHAPTER EIGHT

# The Man Who Stopped the Wind

## EMPEDOCLES

WHILE HERACLITUS MAY HAVE BEEN the least loved Greek sage of his time, Empedocles was probably the most popular. He was such an inspiring lecturer the Greeks called him "the father of public speaking." His generous spirit and remarkable healing ability helped clinch his reputation. Empedocles was born in Sicily, near the beginning of the fifth century B.C.E., and was named after his famous grandfather, who had won top honors at the Olympics. We're told he was a millionaire and that he had flashy taste in clothes.

Empedocles was a passionate democrat in an era when most wealthy men didn't care much for the working class, or hoi polloi, as the rich and powerful sneeringly called them. Empedocles, however, was a crusader. When he saw powerful men bullying the defenseless poor, he took them to court and prosecuted them.

Empedocles was willing to reach deep into his pockets to help others. When a plague threatened the population of Selinus, on the southwest coast of Sicily, he donated the huge sum needed to build two large drainage channels to divert the polluted streams infecting the Selinus River. It ended the plague.

On another occasion the citizens of Acragas, a town not far

from Selinus, complained that an "ill wind" blowing through a cleft in a nearby mountain was making them ill. (It's hard to say now whether the wind was the real cause of their problem; however, scientists today admit that winds carrying an excess of positively charged ions can in fact negatively affect health.) Empedocles spearheaded a massive effort to stop the wind. According to one version of the story, he purchased a huge number of animal hides, had them stitched together, and "sewed up" the cleft in the mountain. This earned him the epithet "the Wind-Stayer."

In another famous incident, Empedocles revived a woman who had been in a deep coma for a month. Word spread that he had raised a dead woman (good stories get even better the more they're repeated). As a healer this "miracle worker" had his work cut out for him: he was continually urging people to recognize the value of hygiene, especially frequent bathing, at a time when cleanliness was not a high priority for most folks. Yet Empedocles was as much a spiritual healer as a physician. Once he spotted a young man who was beside himself with rage, about to attack another fellow who'd offended him. Empedocles started strumming soothingly on a lyre. The soft melody calmed the young man, who later became one of Empedocles' foremost disciples.

You may remember I stated earlier that the Pythagoreans were famous for using music to help people who were mentally disturbed. The fact that Empedocles turned to a lyre to defuse a potentially dangerous situation was no coincidence. Ancient biographers report that he had studied for some time with Pythagorean teachers, as well as with the Persian Magi.

Like the Pythagoreans, Empedocles was a vegetarian. The sage was as much concerned for the welfare of animals as he was for that of his fellow human beings. He wrote of a time "when all animals were tame and the flame of friendship between us and all other creatures burned brightly." He spoke of eating flesh as "pure cruelty," a crime tantamount to cannibalism because animals are our kin. He ardently denounced animal sacrifices, writing of an idyllic time "when people didn't worship Ares or Zeus or Poseidon, but instead honored the Great Goddess. They propitiated her with beautiful paintings and figurines, fragrant oils and incense, and libations of liquid honey. In those days altars weren't drenched with the blood of murdered animals!"

## Exile on Earth

In his role as spiritual counselor, Empedocles strongly recommended meditation. "You must plunge beneath your crowded thoughts and calmly contemplate the higher realities with pure, focused attention. If you do this, a state of inspired serenity will remain with you throughout your life. It will shape your character and help you in so many different ways. But if you direct your attention to the trivial things most people obsess about, the silly nonsense that dulls their minds, you'll just acquire more objects, which you'll only lose anyway."

He also cautioned his audiences against a short-term vision of life. "The wise never imagine that a man lives only for one lifetime, and before and afterward doesn't exist at all." Empedocles saw the soul in Orphic terms. "Divine beings, who through their own error fall under the power of fear and delusion, are forced by eternal law to wander for long cycles, taking birth in mortal bodies, exchanging suffering in one type of body for suffering in another. I'm one of these exiles myself, wandering far from my heavenly source, having mistakenly put my faith in this violent, crazy world."

None of us ever feels completely at home in the material world, Empedocles complained. These physical bodies we're forced to wear feel cumbersome and unnatural to our souls, like an itchy new suit that doesn't quite fit. Without our permission our body gets sick, ages, and dies. Something about it just doesn't feel right; it's not really who we are. But the sages see through the cycle of birth and death. Speaking of the great master Pythagoras, Empedocles wrote in a famous poem:

> There was long ago a man of immense knowledge,
> whose every action resonated with wisdom.
> He was able to grasp everything he reached for
> not with his hands but with his mind.
> He remembered himself for ten or twenty lifetimes.

Lasting happiness and peace come to those "who have gained the wealth of divine understanding." They realize that the divine "isn't something you can see with your eyes or hold in your hands; it doesn't have a face or feet or gender. It is pure consciousness, whose awareness extends throughout the entire cosmos."

"Divine being," he wrote, "is without beginning or end, is nothing but consciousness in any direction, and eternally rejoices in the encircling silence."

It is our task, according to Empedocles, to reclaim this divine awareness, which was lost when we forgot our undying Inner Self and identified completely with a body instead. The sages who have attained Self-realization regain their state as pure spiritual beings, and "have no more part in human sorrow or weariness."

Wherever he went Empedocles attracted enormous crowds. They came to him for healing and for spiritual guidance, or simply to catch a glimpse of the man who'd become a living legend. According to Empedocles the highest professions were the physician, poet, statesman, and spiritual teacher. Clearly, he was all four.

## Leaping into Volcanoes

Empedocles was the most colorful of the Greek masters—brilliant, passionate, flamboyant, deeply caring, and unburdened by modesty. Yet no part of his story is more spectacular than the ending. If the legend is true, at around the age of sixty he and a group of friends climbed Mount Aetna to perform a spiritual practice. (Special rituals were commonly held on Aetna during those periods when the volcano was relatively quiet and participants could approach the crater without burning to death.) When they were finished, the rest of the group started back down the mountain. Empedocles lingered behind. Later that night people reported a brilliant flash of light near the top of the peak.

At daybreak the master still had not rejoined his friends. They searched for him everywhere, but all they ever found was one of his sandals, lying at the edge of the steaming crater. From that day to this, the picture of Empedocles leaping ecstatically into the volcano remains one of the most heart-stopping images of antiquity.

Today Empedocles is primarily remembered as the Greek philosopher who said that nature is made of four elements (earth, water, fire, and air) and two forces (attraction and repulsion, which he described as "love" and "conflict"). Fascinatingly to those of us interested in yoga philosophy, sometimes he referred to a fifth element, aether—a very rarified form of air. Yoga students know that according to Sankhya, the oldest philosophical system of India, there are twenty-four elements, beginning at the most material level with earth, water, fire, air, and aether *(akasha)*. The Sankhya yogis don't end there, however, but trace numerous more elements too subtle to be perceived by the physical senses. These less-dense elements can and often are experienced during higher states of awareness. A twenty-fifth level of reality, completely outside the realm of matter, is consciousness itself.

Because the beginning of Sankhya predates Empedocles by many centuries, it's tempting to speculate that Empedocles was exposed to at least the rudiments of Indian doctrine, perhaps through his Persian mentors. That both the Greek and Hindu systems should begin with identical elements seems like an awfully big coincidence.

Let's turn now to another famous Greek who we're specifically told actually did visit India: Democritus of Abdera.

# CHAPTER NINE

# Atoms and the Void

## DEMOCRITUS

THE ANCIENTS CALLED DEMOCRITUS "the prince of philosophers."
He was most likely born in northern Greece sometime around
460 B.C. He lived, according to at least one report, for more than
a hundred years, and wrote close to sixty books. His insights into
the structure of matter and the formation of galaxies demonstrate
that the greatest of all scientific laboratories may in fact be the
human mind.

Democritus' father was an avid student of the Magi, the brilliant astrologer priests of Persia, and entertained them in his home
as often as possible. From these mentors Democritus learned
astronomy and theology. After his parents died he used his substantial inheritance to travel through much of the civilized world
then known to the Greeks. We are told he made his way south to
Egypt to study geometry with the priests there. Democritus was an
enthusiastic fan of Pythagorean mathematics and may have been
motivated to visit Egypt by the fact that Pythagoras had studied
there a century earlier.

Democritus also headed east in order to study in greater
depth with the Magi and the Chaldeans. Then, according to the
historian Diogenes Laërtes, he continued on to India. Did he

meet the Vaisheshika physicists there? These were the Hindu masters who were already teaching a sophisticated version of atomic theory and who speculated brilliantly on the nature of time and space. Let's pause to consider a new theory that was just beginning to develop in Greece, and then we'll return to India.

## The New Paradigm

Back in Greece a controversial new theoretical paradigm was taking shape. Anaxagoras of Clazomenae (in western Turkey) was claiming that matter, though infinitely divisible, could form molecules. He was a deeply spiritual man who taught that consciousness, called *nous*, shaped the vast chaotic mass of primal matter into the form of the universe we recognize today. He spent much of his life in Athens, a civic-minded city. Once he was asked why he didn't take a more active role in public affairs—didn't he care about his homeland? "I care a great deal about my *true* home," he answered, pointing to the heavens.

Anaxagoras' views on the precession of the equinoxes are fascinating. The precession is caused by the Earth's wobble, which makes the north celestial pole drift dramatically over the millennia. (While Polaris is the North Star today, around thirteen thousand years ago the star Vega enjoyed that honor at the apex of the sky. It's because of this celestial motion that the spring equinox, which currently occurs in Pisces, will shift into the constellation Aquarius in another four centuries.) Anaxagoras was convinced that the north celestial pole once lay at the zenith, the very center of the dome of the sky. As the cosmos spun on its axis, it began to tilt more and more widely, eventually reaching its current lopsided position in the northern corner of heaven. He was the first Greek we know of to teach a version of the New Age idea of a "pole shift."

Anaxagoras' theories about the nature of the universe cost

him his life. It didn't help that he had Persian friends, perhaps even Persian teachers, at a time when the Persian emperor, Xerxes, obviously had plans to attack Athens. Anaxagoras was accused of impiety (he had claimed, for example, that the Sun was a ball of molten metal, not a god). This was a serious charge in Athens in those days, and he was sentenced to death. No less an attorney than Pericles, the greatest statesman in Greek history, defended him in court. It was the ancient Greek equivalent of the Scopes Trial in the twentieth-century United States, when lawyers defended Darwin's theory of evolution. Pericles won the case.

Even though he was now free, Anaxagoras was a broken man. He was so humiliated by the ordeal that, tragically, he committed suicide. But his idea of infinitesimally small pieces of matter had taken hold. Democritus, whose mind was truly encyclopedic, was well aware of these new ideas.

What if Anaxagoras was wrong, Democritus wondered, and you could *not* keep dividing matter into smaller bits indefinitely? What if there was a smallest nugget that just didn't get any smaller? Not through the will of an infinite mind but simply through mechanical forces, these tiny "atoms" might combine to create the cosmos. Here at last was an explanation for why the world is the way it is that made sense to him.

According to Democritus, all that exists are atoms and empty space. Everything in the universe, including us, is made up of an infinite number of tiny, solid particles and the space between them. Worlds come into being as these atoms jostle together, and dissolve as these same atoms shake apart. From beginningless time atoms have had an inherent motion, causing them to collide and the universe to revolve.

The world process was mechanical but not completely random. It was driven by a force Democritus called "necessity," meaning every event had inevitable concrete effects. This accounted for the laws of nature. A particular type of atom colliding with another would either temporarily link with it, owing to their compatible "shapes, sizes, positions, and arrangements," or would push it away if the two atoms had no way to latch together.

Democritus also taught that "there are numberless worlds beside our own. They differ in size. Some are closer to each other; others are more isolated. Some of these worlds sustain life; others are barren." Democritus' description of the night sky is so far ahead of his time, it's nearly impossible to believe he wasn't using a telescope. We know the Egyptians already had lenses at least as far back as 2500 B.C.E.—archaeologists have found lenses in Egypt dating back to the First Dynasty. Scientists like Democritus who had studied in Egypt may well have had access to low-magnitude telescopes.

## Atoms in India

Democritus was a prolific writer. His many books included treatises on optics, Pythagoras, Babylonian scriptures, Chaldean doctrines, the precession of the equinoxes, and even nutrition, the arts, music, divination, and numerous other topics attesting to his broad interests. What a tragedy all these books have been lost! What he is remembered for today, of course, is refining and popularizing atomic theory.

By the time the Greeks started batting around the idea of atoms, atomic theory was already old news in India. (Hindu atomism goes back long before the beginning of both Buddhism and Jainism, around 500 B.C.E.) It's tempting to speculate that Democritus was exposed to Vaisheshika, the Hindu atomic doctrine, while he was in India, or even as a young boy in northern Greece. Vaisheshika was such a dominant philosophical school in India it's hard to believe that news about it hadn't spread beyond the subcontinent. Educated Persians, perhaps even the Magi who taught Democritus when he was a boy, may have been aware of it. There are dramatic differences between Indian and Greek atomism, however. Vaisheshika theorists never wrote spirit out of reality, as Democritus tried to do. For them the full range of phenomena humans typically experience—including psychic phenomena—just can't be explained without factors beyond the gross physical elements, such as mind and consciousness. In his frank materialism, Democritus was actually much closer to the Charvakas, the Indian materialists, than the Vaisheshikas. The Charvakas reasoned that matter is the only reality and that consciousness is no more than a specific aggregate of physical elements. Like Democritus, they believed the "soul" is nothing more than a conscious body. The idea that Democritus may have borrowed some of his theoretical insights from the Hindus is certainly tantalizing.

What, then, did Democritus have to offer Greeks interested in the spiritual life? Democritus rejected the existence of spirit, but not the importance of ethics. Tranquility, he wrote, comes from contentment. People should be happy with what they have, not aspire to more, which only fosters envy and dissatisfaction. Those who feel they are suffering should look to those who suffer worse than they and count their blessings.

Happiness and good health are nurtured by a balanced life-style, he advised. One should not be lazy, but overwork isn't so good either. One should enjoy life but not overindulge, which would only compromise one's health.

Moral behavior should be embraced as a result of the prompting of one's own conscience, not because of fear of the law. We don't know much about Democritus' politics, but he is supposed to have said, "It's better to live in poverty in a democracy than in luxury under tyranny."

True well-being, Democritus felt, is measured not by how much pleasure you experience but by how much serenity. When the soul is calm and strong it becomes unshakable and is no longer subject to delusion or fear. To test his ability to remain tranquil under any circumstances, Democritus would spend long hours alone in a cemetery, rather like some Hindu tantrics.

Democritus was notoriously thrifty, yet even so his inheritance couldn't last forever, especially since he had spent enormous sums on his extensive travels. (I would love to have a copy of his book *A Voyage around the World,* but it's long since lost.) By the time he returned from India he was penniless and had to be supported by one of his brothers. There was actually a law at that time that if a son squandered his inheritance he couldn't be buried in his native city. Wanting to prove he hadn't simply wasted his time and money over the years, Democritus read his masterwork, *The World System,* out loud in the public forum. His fellow citizens were so impressed they awarded him a small fortune (cities provided grants for eminent thinkers in those days) and set up a bronze statue of him, honoring him as one of their most accomplished citizens. Considering that not much earlier, Anaxagoras had been dragged into court for beliefs far less radical than those of Democritus, this award was a real tribute to Democritus' skill as a scientist and educator.

## The Atomic Fallout

The immediate response to Democritus' teachings wasn't always warm. Diogenes of Apollonia (late fifth century B.C.E.) questioned how a brilliantly ordered cosmos could develop by chance. Something had obviously directed matter in the best of all possible ways in order to create such an elegant and seamlessly functioning universe. He felt this just couldn't occur unless the ordering principle manipulating the world process was intelligent. There *had* to be something higher than atoms and the void. Most Greek philosophers agreed with Diogenes.

Epicurus—perhaps the single-most controversial Greek philosopher in antiquity (circa 341–270 B.C.E.)—however, pushed atomism to its logical limits. He explicitly taught that consciousness is nothing more than the interplay of atoms in a physical body. (Indian atomists would have considered this view extremely simplistic.) Therefore, he taught, there is no life after death and the gods—if they exist—don't bother themselves with our concerns.

At any rate, thinking about things too much gains us nothing, Epicurus preached. We should work with the evidence the senses present to us rather than searching in vain for deeper meaning where none in fact exists. The only purpose of life that makes any sense is to enjoy ourselves. Far from encouraging his students to live life in the fast lane, though, Epicurus encouraged them to adopt a life of moderation, since overindulgence would only make them sick.

Though the citizens of his hometown considered Democritus a genius, one particularly influential Greek was totally disgusted with him. Plato not only believed dismissing the spiritual dimensions of life was philosophically myopic, he also feared that a godless, soulless vision of the universe would lead inevitably to a spiritual wasteland. Today an updated version of atomic theory dominates modern consciousness. We're now in a position to decide for ourselves whether Plato was right.

CHAPTER TEN

# The Man Who Lost a Continent

PLATO

IT'S A TALE THAT HAS HAUNTED the Western imagination for twenty-four hundred years. Solon, Athens' great lawgiver, was on a pilgrimage to Sais in northern Egypt, where the priests warmly received him. His reputation as one of Greece's great sages had opened doors for him that normally were closed to Greek gawkers and sightseers. The priests may also have been impressed by the fact that their illustrious guest was the pre-eminent citizen of Athens, their sister city. Sais too was dedicated to the goddess Athena, though she was called Neith in the Egyptian language. In those days advanced societies didn't consider other cultures' deities to be false gods. They recognized them as their own gods under different names.

Solon told the priests stories from Greek history going all the way back to the Great Flood, which only Deucalion and his wife, Pyrrha, had survived, huddled in an ark that came aground on Mount Parnassus. He was stunned by their response. "Solon, you Greeks are like children. You don't remember your own past. It's not surprising you know so little since your culture was almost completely destroyed.

"You have a myth about Apollo's son Phaeton, who tried

to drive his father's chariot across the sky but crashed into the Earth instead, scorching everything in his path. This sounds like a fable to you, but events like this really happen. At certain intervals bodies that sweep through the heavens do strike the Earth, causing incalculable destruction. At other times enormous floods sweep away entire populations. The deluge that Deucalion and Pyrrha survived was only the latest of many similar disasters. Fortunately, here in Egypt, we've been shielded from these catastrophes. Therefore we've been able to preserve the history of our people, going back many thousands of years. You Greeks, however, remember back only a few generations. Yet if you knew the truth about your distant ancestors, how they fought off a huge invading army that threatened us all nine thousand years ago, you would be extremely proud."

Solon was astonished and asked to hear more. One priest went on to explain that long ago an aggressive civilization centered off the western coast of Spain—on a continent "as large as North Africa and West Asia put together"—had dominated much of the ancient world. The Greeks alone managed to hang onto their freedom and with extraordinary courage drove the invaders back into the sea. But they had no sooner freed the enslaved peoples of Europe and Africa than "in one terrible day and night," a flood of staggering proportions swept away their world. It drowned most of the Greeks and entirely submerged the original homeland of the invading armies. This vanished continent, which once flourished "outside the pillars of Hercules" in the Atlantic Ocean, had been called Atlantis, the priest claimed.

Did Atlantis really exist? Records confirming this story have never been found in Egypt. The only original source we have for the tale are two essays by a Greek intellectual named Aristocles, born in Athens around 427 B.C.E.

Aristocles had a broad forehead, which earned him the

nickname by which he is known to history, Plato, from the Greek word for "wide." Some say the epithet refers instead to the breadth of his phenomenally active mind. He was physically large and strong—he took up amateur wrestling as a young man. There was an artist in him too: he enjoyed painting and writing poetry. But there was a deeply sober and thoughtful turn to Plato's personality. His biographers specifically make the point that, unlike many other rich young men of that time, and ours, he was no party animal. Once he was so disgusted with his drunken friends that he demanded they take a good, hard look in a mirror, presuming the shocking sight of their faces distorted by drink would cure them of their addiction to alcohol. Unlike them he was orderly, industrious, and self-disciplined. He condemned oversleeping as a terrible waste of time and gambling as a pernicious vice. He was often off by himself, preferring solitude to the company of fools.

We're told Plato rarely laughed, which is surprising since his numerous surviving essays are full of sly humor. One day an Athenian comedian made fun of his pedantic habit of painstakingly defining his terms. A human, Plato had said, was a "featherless biped," meaning we're the only creatures other than birds who routinely walk on two legs. The comedian held up a plucked chicken and announced, "Look, everyone, here's Plato's ideal man!" Plato responded by amending his definition. "A human," he wryly corrected himself, "is a featherless biped with flat fingernails."

Plato was one of the finest writers in history, but apparently he was not a popular speaker in his own day. We're told that during one of his lectures the students were so bored that one by one they got up and left, leaving only a young man named Aristotle still conscientiously taking notes. It didn't help that Plato's voice was high and feminine, almost birdlike, which may have irritated audiences. But whatever skills he lacked in public speaking he more than made up for with his pen: Plato's voluminous writings are universally acknowledged as masterpieces of Greek literature. And the school he started in his house in Athens, called simply "the Academy," would educate some of the greatest minds in European history for the next thousand years.

It's tempting to wonder whether, as he sat jotting down his ideas, Plato had even the faintest inkling how massively influential his work would become. He was in fact deeply ambitious, and may well have written with one eye trained on future generations. Plato would succeed in becoming the most famous of all ancient Western sages, with one possible exception: his own teacher, the maddeningly inquisitive gadfly named Socrates.

## The Swan Song

Socrates claimed he'd dreamed of a swan that dropped out of the sky. It extended its magnificent plumes, majestically shook its wings, and let out a piercing cry before leaping back into heaven. The next day he met the teenager who would change the world. When Plato first introduced himself, his voice high-pitched like the bird in the dream, Socrates knew he'd found his swan.

If Plato was a swan, Socrates was—notoriously—a gadfly. He would wander the streets of Athens seeking out its most respected intellectuals, politicians, and artists and ask them simple questions. These questions sounded innocent enough, which lured more than one pompous aristocrat into running on about his views on justice, love, or art. Probing with disingenuous questions that cloaked inexorable logic, Socrates would lead his victims into a mass of self-contradictions, making one after another of Athens' leading citizens look like idiots.

Young men like Plato followed Socrates on his rounds. It was so much fun to watch their mentor humiliate the city's authority figures. At the same time Socrates' habit of questioning absolutely everything—from what people meant by virtue, to what makes something desirable, to what constitutes a just society—made Plato realize we humans know far less than we imagine we do. If we can't trust what the authorities tell us, what really *is* true?

Finally, Athens' leading citizens had enough. They arrested Socrates for "impiety" (lack of respect for the gods) and "corrupting the city's youth." Both charges were wild exaggerations, but they carried the death penalty. It's unlikely the authorities really wanted to kill the old man. They expected him to flee and no doubt set up shop in some other city, funded by his numerous young, well-heeled admirers. They really didn't care what he did, as long as he did it somewhere else. As they expected, Socrates' disciples immediately set in motion an escape plan. But then something completely unanticipated happened. *Socrates refused to run.*

Socrates was not a criminal. He was a brilliant thinker and an indefatigable pest who made powerful people look ridiculous. But his final act, his acceptance of the death sentence they imposed, made Athens' top citizens look not just like idiots but assassins. He forced them to deal with the consequences of their unjust act and showed them how a man with a clear conscience meets death.

The last day of Socrates' life is chronicled in Plato's ultimate classic, *Phaedo.* Socrates had always refused to accept anything simply because somebody said it was true; he'd subjected every claim to merciless analysis. Now in the last few hours of his life he turned his attention to the final, most perplexing question of all: Is there life after death?

Socrates carefully weighed the arguments for and against the immortality of the soul, and admitted this mystery couldn't be resolved by reason alone. But beyond reason there was something more, the soul's intuitive knowledge of itself, that hinted at an answer. "I honestly believe there is something more for those who have died, something far better for the good than for the wicked," he concluded.

"There is a legend," Socrates mused, "that our souls continue on in another world after leaving this one, but eventually they return. They say the living come from the dead and the dead come from the living. We're thrown back into this world like criminals thrown into prison, chained by our desires to the things we still crave in the physical world. But if our soul devotes itself to the pursuit of wisdom, then when it leaves this body it abides forever in a subtler state.

"When the soul dives into itself, it discovers a state that's absolutely changeless. How does it do this? It needs only to free itself from every mental disturbance. The soul can untie itself from desire for the passing things of this world by constantly contemplating the higher world and drawing strength and inspiration from it. Then at death it is freed from the suffering of human life, and abides in a permanent state worthy of a divinity.

"They say when a swan realizes its time of death is approaching, it sings more sweetly than ever before. Some people say it's singing with grief. But birds don't sing when they're in pain; they only sing when they're full of joy. The swan knows it's returning to Apollo, the god it has always devotedly served, and sings with joy at the wonder it knows awaits it in the world to come. I believe I have lived my life in service of the same god, and look forward to entering his light."

The executioner arrived with a bowl of deadly hemlock, the lethal injection of that era. Watching Socrates willingly drink the poison, his disciples started to sob uncontrollably. "I sent the women away because they couldn't control their emotions, and now look how you're behaving! Pull yourselves together!" Socrates commanded. "It's important to die in an atmosphere of tranquility."

The sage walked around his cell for several minutes till his legs began to feel heavy. Then he lay down on his cot and covered his face with a cloth. In a few more moments the master passed through the gate of death and discovered for himself the answer to his final question.

## Academic Life

The death of his mentor in 399 B.C.E. must have been devastating for Plato. He went on to write dozens of short stories called "dialogues," featuring Socrates as the main speaker. These philosophical discourses were probably largely fictional but reflected the huge impact Socrates had on his life.

But Socrates was by no means the only influence on Plato. The colors of Parmenides, Heraclitus, and Empedocles are all refracted through the prism of his writings, as well as the blazing light of Pythagoras. Plato traveled a great deal after Socrates' passing and lived for a while in southern Italy, where he studied with the Pythagorean teachers who still lived there. The Pythagorean preoccupation with music theory and astronomy, and with the mathematical ratios that underpinned both these sciences, are clearly evident in his essays. Plato eventually was accused of publishing the secret teachings of esoteric groups. This type of copyright infringement was still a serious charge in his day. In earlier centuries he might have been executed for it.

Today we can only be thankful that Plato had the courage and foresight to include at least some of the "secret doctrines" of his era in his dialogues; otherwise we might never have known the amazing extent to which the Greeks cherished mystical beliefs similar to the Hindus'. Plato did make a halfhearted attempt to be discreet about this, rarely specifically identifying his teachers but referring to them in the vaguest of terms (for example, "wise men and women," "someone I met," "the followers of Orpheus," or simply "the ancients").

We know that like other well-educated men of the time, Plato embarked for Egypt, where he no doubt eagerly sought out the priests' secret doctrines and histories. We're told he also wanted to study with the Zoroastrian Magi, but the rapidly deteriorating political relations between the Greeks and Persians ruled out that possibility.

Plato's interests were more than theoretical. He was obsessed with politics. He passionately wanted to translate his ideas about a just and enlightened society into practical reality. He believed that a civilization headed by philosopher-kings—men wise, strong, and selfless enough to control the population for the betterment of all—was the solution to many of humanity's worst problems. He was no democrat, observing that many people are just too stupid to be allowed self-rule.

Like a surprising number of other early Greek thinkers, Plato believed that if males shared their wives and children in common, society would be the stronger for it. In our own day, many of us having experimented with communal living, it's easy to see how naive Plato was being. He never married or had children himself, and didn't seem to appreciate the extent to which familial bonding and romantic jealousy drive human psychology. At any rate, Plato traveled to Syracuse in Sicily at least three times, where two local rulers seemed interested in helping him establish his utopia, but his efforts came to nothing.

Plato died in 347 B.C.E. at the age of eighty-one. He passed away at a wedding celebration, though we don't know the details. By that time the Academy he founded had become a huge success. It had numerous teachers and a varied curriculum, making it one of the first true universities we know of in the Western world. If you studied there in a previous incarnation, you might have taken classes in astronomy, mathematics, anatomy, philosophy, or political science. In fact our word *academic* comes from the name of Plato's school.

## Plato's Ideas

What did Plato teach? His most famous idea was the concept of ideas. Plato noted that there are two classes of things: those we perceive with our senses, which are constantly changing, and those we conceive with our minds, which never change. For example, you'll see millions of circular objects throughout your life, such as round stones or cart wheels, and obviously none of these things lasts forever. But the *concept* of a circle never changes. For all eternity a circle will remain a two-dimensional object in which the distance from its center to any point on its circumference is the same. You will never find an absolutely perfect circle in nature, but the *idea* of a perfect circle is easy to imagine.

For Plato the world of ideas was more fundamentally real than anything in the physical universe. Everyone understands the idea of justice, though true justice eludes us in the material world. Everyone has an idealized picture of flawless beauty or true love, yet beauty in our world fades and relationships end. Even though we don't see perfect justice or perfect beauty or perfect love in the world, or even a perfect circle, still we intuitively know what they are. They're completely real in our minds.

According to Plato, the universe is made from ideas or archetypes like the circle, which have been projected into matter. They shape the formless sea of primal matter into a living, coherent cosmos. So, for example, every horse you'll ever see is, in a sense, a specific manifestation of the horse archetype, impressed on material substance that otherwise wouldn't assume any shape at all. Today many believe these regulatory patterns are somehow encoded in our DNA. Plato located them in the mind of God.

Our physical senses don't have access to the "original templates," only to their images in matter. But we can know the archetypes with our minds. The sages contemplate the eternal objects in the inner world, which unlike objects here are perfect and undying. Contemplation of these ideals brings us closer to an understanding of God.

## Leaving the Cave

Plato likened the world to a dark cave in which we are born, live, and die. We're tied down so we can see only the wall in front of us. On that wall we see nothing but the play of shadows, yet those shadows are the whole of reality for us. Imagine that one man pulls loose and finds his way through the dark tunnels out of the cave. The first moment he steps into the daylight he'll be blinded by the Sun, but as his eyes adjust he'll be amazed at the spectacular world he sees around him.

Now what if that man reenters the cave and tells his friends about the amazing sights he's seen and encourages them to escape too? Most people in the cave won't believe him; they'll think he's either crazy or a liar. They may even try to kill him, because they feel their entire worldview is being threatened by his stories. Plato noted that this is often the fate of philosophers and mystics who explore the inner world and then try to tell others about it.

Why then did God create this material world, the "dark cave" we all live in? For Plato, God is the highest good and beauty and truth. Because he is absolutely perfect he can never be subject to selfishness, anger, or jealousy. Instead he seeks to share his pure goodness with all other creatures. *We were placed here to become like him.*

By leaving the cave and entering the world above, like the

free man in the story, we begin approaching the Supreme Being, embracing within ourselves more and more of his beauty and goodness.

The universe, Plato taught, is not just a conglomeration of physical elements. It is an actual living entity that regulates itself, that has a soul. It is not God (who has no physical form), so it can't be perfect; but it was created by God, so it is as near perfection as it's possible for a material entity to be. The orbits of the stars and the magic of music are examples of near perfection we can contemplate in order to draw nearer to God's perfect, transcendent being.

## Searching and Learning

How did different kinds of creatures come into being? Incredibly, Plato taught an early version of the theory of evolution, though his vision of the order of evolution was the exact opposite of Darwin's. Plato guessed that humans were the first creatures created by the angels God had assigned to design the world. These angels foresaw that in the future most human souls would refuse to live out their full potential as spiritual beings. Therefore they would need to be reborn into other types of bodies in order to fulfill their lower desires. And so, for example, the first humans were given fingernails that could later be modified into hoofs or claws.

But it's spiritual evolution that really matters. Plato said, "The soul itself is immortal. The priests and priestesses have always said this, and it's both beautiful and true. At one time a soul's association with a particular body comes to an end, and at another time it is reborn in another body, but the soul itself never perishes. Therefore it's imperative that we live pure lives." He continued, "What ruins our lives is injustice and senseless aggression. What allows us to flourish is justice and a way of life that is sensible and self-controlled."

Plato didn't believe any soul purposely chose to be evil. "A man becomes evil because of bad habits he developed due to the way he was raised. It is the parents, not the child, who should be blamed. However, if a man discovers evil in himself he must do everything he can to escape these faults, reeducating himself and cultivating better habits."

Plato was an avid exponent of a lifestyle we today would characterize as "holistic." "The intellectually oriented person," he wrote, "must give his body its due and get enough exercise. The physically oriented person must give his soul its due by exercising his mind and educating himself." He was not impressed by people who tried to extend their longevity with one form of medication or another, noting even then the dangerous side effects of drugs. "Prolong your life by faithfully maintaining a healthy daily regimen," he advised.

Plato believed we have all lived innumerable lives "searching and learning." In this life much of what we imagine we're learning for the first time in fact we're simply remembering from a previous existence in this world or some other, such as the archetypal realm itself.

We have no cause to complain when we meet severe challenges in life, he said. "If we believe everything that happens is the will of the gods, and that the gods are good and love us, then we must admit the difficulties we face are sent to us for our own good. What could these painful experiences be but just punishment for mistakes we made in our past lives?"

Plato said that just as people see their whole life flash before their eyes when they leave their bodies at death, so souls first entering a body also briefly glimpse the entire life they're about to experience. That may explain the sensation of déjà vu, or the sense people sometimes have that a particular event in their lives is preordained. In fact, he taught that people actually choose many of the events they're going to experience before they enter their next physical body, so that they can work out their destiny and continue to grow spiritually.

## The Divine Plato

For centuries after Plato's death, his essays—along with the poems of Homer and Hesiod—were quoted as sacred scripture. Plato was called "divine" because he seemed to have a direct channel to the hidden dimensions of the cosmos. And perhaps he did. "I can tell you what I've heard the ancients said, but they alone know the truth," he wrote. As a result of the cultural catastrophe that occurred several centuries earlier, the Greeks had lost their connection with the ancient wisdom tradition still preserved in other cultures such as Egypt, Persia, and India. Plato put them back in touch with the sacred heritage of the world.

We have lost almost all the writings of the great minds of Western antiquity. Plato is a dramatic exception: more than forty of the essays attributed to him have survived to the present day. His dialogues represent some of the best thinking and most inspiring insights of the ancient Greek world. And most importantly, his spiritual teachings link us—as they once did his Greek disciples—with Pythagorean masters, Orphic mystics, and Egyptian priests whose works have been entirely lost, if they were ever written down at all.

In the early sixth century C.E., however, Christian leaders, eager to exterminate the pagan traditions, closed the Academy and ended its by then thousand-year-old lineage. Fortunately, Plato's writings survived in the Islamic world and were reintroduced to Europe in the fifteenth century. At that time Plato's name once again became synonymous with mystical wisdom and spiritual lore. From then till the early twentieth century, people in the Western world could not consider themselves fully educated unless they had read Plato.

As the twentieth century wore on, however, and a more purely materialistic tradition reminiscent of Democritus took over our modern academies, Plato once again lost his hold on the Western imagination. The very questions Plato asked most urgently (What is the nature of the soul? What happens after death? What can we know about the Supreme Being?) were dismissed as the useless inquiries of a superstitious mind. For Plato, the spiritual world we can see only with the mind was the real world; for scientists and academicians today, that world doesn't even exist.

What a shame our culture has lost Plato for a second time.

## Searching for Atlantis

But what about Atlantis? This tantalizing tale is the one portion of Plato's legacy in which the public today is still interested. Could the story of the antediluvian continent have some basis in fact? According to Plato, Socrates' friend Critias was the great-grandson of Solon, the Greek statesman who purportedly first learned about Atlantis from the Egyptians. If this is true, there is a chance that Solon's account could have been passed down through Critias to Plato.

Plausible theories have been offered in recent decades suggesting that Plato's tale of a submerged civilization was loosely based on the destruction of the island of Thera in the Mediterranean, or of the sunken city of Tantalis near modern Manisa in Turkey. (The tops of some buildings in Tantalis were still visible under the surface of the Black Lake in Plato's time.) If we understand Plato to have meant that although the city of Atlantis was just beyond the Strait of Gibraltar, its *sphere of influence* was as large as North Africa and West Asia put together, then the city may still lie in the shallow coastal waters off western Spain.

Enthusiastic seekers have also placed Atlantis in North or Central America, and even in the Andean plateau in South America. Southeast Asia has been suggested, as has Britain, along with the Azores in the middle of the Atlantic Ocean. Perhaps the Atlanteans were founders of ancient Anatolian cities such as Çatal Hüyük, or maybe their homeland lies beneath the Black Sea. One extremely charming book even finds Atlantis in eastern Antarctica! One conclusion seems inescapable: you can find Atlantis anywhere you look.

I certainly don't know the answer to this maddening mystery, though it's always struck me as eerie that Plato described dramatic Earth changes 11,500 years ago, exactly when the Pleistocene epoch ended and huge geological shifts did in fact occur. It's most likely, though, that he wove a spectacular yarn from tangled legends of various sunken kingdoms, colored in with idealistic notions of utopian politics and Greek nobility, skillfully adding the esoteric mathematics of Pythagoras—these allusions being so subtle only another initiate would catch his drift.

There's another possibility I'd like to suggest. It's impossible for anyone familiar with ancient Indian literature to miss the parallels between Plato's description of the ringed city of Atlantis and Bhu Mandala, the Hindu cosmological paradigm. It's as if Plato compressed the Hindu cosmos down to city size. If this connection is more than accidental, no one has securely identified the lost continent anywhere on Earth because it actually exists *in the sky*. The bulls and elephants Plato mentions would be the constellations Taurus and Scorpio (Scorpio was pictured as an elephant's head in the Indus Valley). The ten "twin" Atlantean kings Plato mentions would be the ten famous marker stars of antiquity, which were set along the ecliptic.

In ancient Hindu astronomy the word *dvipa* or "continent" represented the concentric sectors of the universe. During the twenty-six-thousand-year course of the precessional cycle, different dvipas, or sectors of space, sink below the celestial equator. Ancient astronomers would then designate a specific date, "one terrible day and night" either on the spring equinox or the winter solstice, when their entire celestial paradigm would have to be discarded in order to accommodate the changing face of the night sky. Old calendars that had been used for generations were now obsolete, though if you waited long enough in the twenty-six-thousand-year cycle, that "continent" would eventually rise again.

Plato says Atlantis was founded by Atlas, the mythical figure who held up the sky. In Egypt, Atlas was represented by the god Shu, who in countless Egyptian paintings holds up heaven with his two upraised arms. Shu may have represented the constellation we call Hercules. (In Greek mythology Hercules took Atlas' place holding up heaven. Incidentally, while today we imagine Hercules upside down in the sky, the Egyptians visualized all their constellations right-side up, so the Greek constellation Hercules' legs were the Egyptian constellation Shu's arms.) Over thousands of years the north celestial pole gradually passed between one of Shu's uplifted "hands" to the other. It truly would have looked as if Shu were holding up the night sky.

The figure of Atlas may represent a dim memory of an earlier era when the constellation Shu dominated the night. Perhaps the sinking of Atlantis represents Atlas' fall from celestial preeminence as the precessional cycle shifted the north celestial pole inexorably away from those stars into the tail of Draco. It's curious that the sector of the sky immediately beneath the horizon is called Atala in Sanskrit.

We do know that Plato was fascinated by astronomy and valued its secrets as central mysteries of the universe. But then Plato wrote so slyly we can find Atlantis anywhere we want or need to—on the earth, under the sea, or among the stars. His most famous student, Aristotle of Stagira—the one still taking notes after all the other students had left—was convinced Atlantis never existed anywhere but in his teacher's lively imagination. Perhaps ultimately Atlantis is simply another of Plato's "ideas," a sunken kingdom that exists only in the fathomless depths of human consciousness.

It's startling how many of Plato's teachings, particularly his descriptions of the soul's wanderings from life to life until it becomes enlightened, sound like they came straight out of the yoga tradition. Even Plato's archetypes have parallels in the Indian tradition, where they were called *samanya*. But it's far more likely that Plato based much of his work on Egyptian models.

Now that you've learned a little about Plato, it's time to discover more about his most successful student.

# CHAPTER ELEVEN

# The Master of Those Who Know

### ARISTOTLE

PROXENUS HAD BIG PLANS for the bright young orphan he was raising. The boy's late father had been a doctor at the court of Amyntas II, the king of Macedon. It may have been from this physician father that the boy inherited an avid enthusiasm for the study of nature: biology, botany, chemistry, and whatever other aspects of the natural world he could explore.

Proxenus had heard there was a new school in Athens called the Academy, headed by a fellow named Plato, where boys could get the best education available in the Greek world. So when Aristotle turned seventeen, that's where Proxenus sent him.

An exceptionally intelligent and curious young man, Aristotle spent the next twenty years in Athens. We don't know how much time he spent in Plato's presence, since the headmaster traveled a great deal, seeking out esoteric knowledge and attempting to establish a utopian city-state. Nevertheless, Aristotle thrived at the Academy and readily accepted Platonic tenets such as reincarnation. However, his deepest interests diverged to some extent from his teacher's. While Plato was primarily focused on the unchanging truths behind the ever-changing world of appearances, Aristotle was fascinated by the complex universe we experience through our senses.

Aristotle's world turned upside down when Plato died in 347 B.C.E. The new king of Macedon, Philip II, was in constant conflict with the Athenians. Although Aristotle was not Macedonian—he was born in the town of Stagira in northern Greece in 384 B.C.E.—the fact that his father had hobnobbed with Macedonian royalty raised suspicions about Aristotle's loyalties. He may have been tiring of theoretical studies anyway and perhaps wanted to spend more time studying anatomy and biology. Or maybe he simply needed to find a job to support his wife and growing family. Whatever his motivation, Aristotle left Athens shortly after Plato's death.

Then in 343 B.C.E. a remarkable opportunity presented itself. King Philip of Macedon had a bright, promising son himself and wanted the best possible education for the thirteen-year-old. He obviously couldn't send him to Plato's Academy since he was at war with Athens, but he could do the next best thing: hire a former student of the Academy as a tutor. Aristotle, whose father had served in the Macedonian court years before, looked like the perfect fit. And that is how Aristotle became the teacher of Philip's feisty son, the young man we remember today as Alexander the Great. I'll have more to say about their tempestuous relationship in a moment.

Eight years later Aristotle returned to Athens and opened an academy of his own just northeast of the city. It was called the Lyceum after a nearby grove dedicated to the god Apollo. Most of the writings of Aristotle we have today were probably originally his or his students' lecture notes. His followers were called the Peripatetics, named after the *peripatoi*, or colonnades, of the building where he taught.

But then in 323 B.C.E., Aristotle was once again driven from the city—his association with the hated Macedonians had indeed been a mixed blessing. The Athenian government charged him with impiety, the same charge for which Socrates, his teacher's teacher, had been executed. It looked like he was being primed for the same fate. Claiming he could not allow Athens to commit a second crime against philosophy, Aristotle fled to Chalcis, on the Greek island of Euboea, where he died a natural death the following year.

## The Sum of All Knowledge

The breadth of Aristotle's scholarship was truly encyclopedic. With the help of his students he compiled a library's worth of information about physics, metaphysics, cosmology, astronomy, meteorology, geology, optics, ethics, politics, rhetoric, poetry, drama, dreams, music, logic, zoology, and medicine. His erudition was so vast that even a thousand years later Dante Alighieri, author of *The Divine Comedy*, hailed him as "the master of those who know."

Aristotle believed it is not enough to sit at home and theorize about the nature of the universe, as most of Plato's other disciples did. Instead he urged his pupils to go out and examine the world in detail so they could make an informed assessment about its particulars. Much of what he and his pupils concluded (for example, that the Earth lay at the center of the universe) we now know was mistaken. This was not yet experimental science as we know it today, but it *was* a robust start to the Western scientific tradition.

Aristotle noted that humans have a great deal in common with animals but that one thing above all distinguishes us from them. *Humans desire to know*—not just to know where we can find our next meal, but how our bodies work, how we can form a better society, what the stars are made of. We take pleasure in knowledge for its own sake.

- Aristotle categorized human knowledge into three types.

- Practical: how to raise crops, build houses, sail ships, and so on
- Ethical: how to live so as to maximize our health and fulfillment
- Theoretical: seeking the ultimate nature of God, the universe, and our own soul

Aristotle wrote extensively on ethics. A happy life, he believed, is a balanced life. It involves walking a middle path between extremes. Between anger on the one hand and slavish fawning on the other lies respect for others and oneself. Between self-indulgence and self-denial lies temperance. Between rashness and cowardice lies courage. We must cultivate the rational part of our nature in order to make wise decisions that allow us to find balance and truly flourish. "To live a good life is not easy," he admitted. "To perform each action to the right degree, at the right time, with the right purpose, and in the right way, is the basis of a noble life."

The best lifestyle of all, however, is a life of contemplation. Metaphysics is the most divine of sciences because it confers not just knowledge, but wisdom. Contemplating that which *is* (God) and that which *is something* (the world) is not only the most sublime way to live, it's the easiest, because a philosopher requires little from the world, only the bare necessities needed to maintain life.

Contemplating what he had learned about nature over the years, Aristotle came to a conclusion strikingly different from that of scientists today. It seemed to him that atoms and the forces that acted on them could not in themselves explain the structure and complexity of the universe and the living things within it. Aristotle was well aware that atomists like Democritus argued that cosmic processes occur randomly. But things that happen by chance don't occur regularly. And we see regularity, not randomness, virtually everywhere we look.

The whole, Aristotle observed, is greater than the sum of its parts. Nature moves toward a goal; it is purposeful. He wasn't saying the universe is guided by a cosmic mind, as Plato believed. Rather, God is the eternal intelligence outside time and space, the final end toward which all of nature inherently aspires.

Where does that leave *us*? Our feelings and thinking processes are generated in the body; when the body dies, they also perish. But there is a part of us that exists beyond our mortal human ego. This supersensory inner being functions purely intuitively and represents a sort of divine intelligence. It's called *nous* in Greek (related to our English word *noetic*). This innermost self survives death but reincarnates if it's still attracted to material life. This view is amazingly similar to the yogic doctrines of India.

It is nearly impossible to exaggerate the enormity of Aristotle's impact on the Western and Islamic worlds. He was considered the supreme authority on physical science until the Renaissance, profoundly influencing Christianity, Judaism, and Islam.

But let's take a closer look at Aristotle's star pupil, whose impact on history was no less immense.

## Alexander's Guru

Though Aristotle was Alexander's teacher, the Indian yogi Kalyana was his guru. It's a remarkable story recorded by Plutarch, Strabo, and other ancient Greek writers.

In the decade before his death in 323 B.C.E., Alexander the Great conquered the world, or at least a sizable portion of the world known to the classical Greeks. Starting from his native Macedonia, he took over much of Greece, then Egypt in the south, and then large tracts of Persia and Central Asia to the east. Alexander took with him a retinue of botanists and zoologists, no doubt at Aristotle's prompting. However, Alexander's relationship with his teacher was not always a happy one. Alexander actually executed Aristotle's nephew for allegedly conspiring to assassinate him. There has long been speculation that Aristotle himself may have been involved in the plot. We'll never know for sure what happened, but it's unmistakably true that many Greeks deeply resented the fact that after conquering Persia, Alexander enthusiastically embraced Eastern culture, clearly preferring it to the West.

Finally, in 327 B.C.E. Alexander marched into what is now Pakistan, determined to conquer India. He literally didn't know what he was getting into; the Greeks' knowledge of geography was so poor they actually mistook the Indus River in the Punjab for the source of the Nile! (They were probably misled by one of the Indian names for the Indus. Hindus called it the Nila, meaning "Blue River.")

But the once-invincible Alexander made little headway in the subcontinent. His men were terrified by the elephants that Hindu troops rode into battle—to the Greeks, they must have seemed like armored tanks. Alexander himself nearly died from wounds sustained in fighting the Hindus, perhaps the most concrete evidence his soldiers had seen that he wasn't invulnerable after all. Fed up with sloshing through the monsoon rain, they wanted to go home.

The effort to conquer India was a total failure—Alexander's first. Yet while he was there he made several important discoveries. First, he found Indians who spoke Greek and were familiar with the Greek gods. Modern Western historians have largely ignored evidence like this of contacts between the Indians and Greeks long before Alexander arrived on the scene.

But even more dramatically, it was here that Alexander met several of India's legendary *sadhus*—ascetic yogis who devote their lives to the exploration of consciousness and its energies. Aristotle had taught him about the external world, and he had set out to conquer it. These yogis, who so astounded the Greeks, had mastered the *inner* world. Another world to conquer! Alexander, like many travelers to India even today, was looking for a guru.

We're told Alexander's men soon met a yogi they called Dadamis—probably a Danda Swami, a Hindu ascetic who owns nothing but a *danda*, or walking stick. Hoping to learn his doctrines, Alexander sent an emissary with this message: "Alexander, son of Zeus and sovereign of the entire Earth, commands you to come at once. If he is pleased with you, you will be richly rewarded. If not, you will die."

"There is only one supreme king," Danda answered calmly, "the one who created light and life. This is the only king I obey, and he abhors war.

"How can this Alexander be supreme ruler as long as he himself is subject to the King of Death? And what can he offer me when my mother the Earth already provides everything I need? I have no possessions I need to guard, so I sleep peacefully at night.

"Alexander can kill my body, but he can't touch my soul. Tell your king that at the time of death each of us is called to account for our deeds. Ask him how he's going to explain the agony of those he has murdered and oppressed. He can tempt those who crave gold, he can terrify those who fear death, but we yogis care for neither. Tell your Alexander he has nothing I want, and I will *not* come to him."

When Alexander heard this reply, he exclaimed, "I conquered the world, but this naked old man has conquered me!"

Alexander also tried approaching a yogi the Greeks called Kalanos (probably Kalyana in Sanskrit), but the elderly sadhu would have nothing to do with him. "Strip naked or I won't say a word to you, not even if God sent you himself!" Kalyana commanded. No doubt he hoped to teach the arrogant young ruler a little humility. Perhaps he was also hinting at the level of renunciation required for real spiritual growth—that one must strip off one's egotism and desires in order to experience the true self within. Luckily for Alexander, one of Kalyana's disciples persuaded the aged master that it was a good thing a Greek emperor had come to India seeking spiritual wisdom. So Kalyana agreed to accompany Alexander back to Greece as his guru.

We don't know the details of Alexander's discipleship, but he probably made a poor student. The young conqueror was a raging alcoholic, uncontrollably addicted to power and its perks. By the time the retreating army reached the province of Persis (today's Fars in Iran), Kalyana had had enough and announced he was leaving his body. He gave away the numerous gifts Alexander had lavished on him and ordered the Greeks to build him a pyre. Then, chanting mantras and wearing only a garland of flowers, Kalyana stepped into the flames. To the Greeks' complete astonishment, he showed no sign of discomfort as the fire consumed his body. Alexander could not control him; to the very last moment, Kalyana was a total master of himself.

Stories like these of the wisdom, renunciation, and unshakable equanimity of the yogis electrified the Greeks, who carried tales of the extraordinary wise men of India back to their homeland.

Some of the Greeks who accompanied Alexander to India apparently decided to become yogis themselves. The most famous of these was Pyrrho of Elis, who lived in India for a year and a half. Returning to Greece, Pyrrho taught that it's not enough to *talk* philosophy as the Greeks so loved to do; one has to *live* it. A true philosopher is at peace with himself and the universe, unaffected by the conditions of his life and the events around him, like the yogis who never surrendered their state of tranquility.

Pyrrho founded a spiritual school called Skepticism, based in part on what he learned in India. He taught his students to be skeptical of—that is, not to accept at face value—knowledge provided by the mind or senses. One point of view explains the world one way, another explains it a different way. Who can tell which is correct? The real truth, he explained, is beyond the reach of rational inquiry. Therefore it is best not to lose oneself in logical analysis but rather to cultivate a state of inner peace, free from craving and attachment. The dramatic similarity between Skeptical tenets and aspects of both Jainism and Madhyamika Buddhism have been delineated by numbers of Western scholars in recent years.

There is a well-known story that one day Pyrrho was attacked by a wild dog and involuntarily leapt back in fear. He ruefully admitted that maintaining perfect tranquility—as Danda had done before Alexander's soldiers and Kalyana had done in the funeral pyre—wasn't so easy. Nevertheless, Pyrrho's example of an ethical yet serene and nonattached lifestyle had a significant impact in Greece. The tradition Pyrrho founded endured in the Western world for centuries.

Now it's time to introduce the Greek sage whose extensive firsthand research led him to insist that, long before Aristotle and Alexander were even born, the great Egyptian civilization had inherited its spiritual wisdom from the yoga masters of India.

# CHAPTER TWELVE

# Apollonius Was Like the Sun

## APOLLONIUS

IT WAS THE FIRST CENTURY C.E. and an aggressive new empire, born in Rome, was imposing its will on the Western world. Amid the glory and the savagery of Roman expansion, a remarkable prophet traveled the length of the empire with a small band of devoted disciples, urging people to live virtuously, abandon greed and luxury, and instead care for the poor and oppressed. He healed the sick, cast out demons, and even, some said, raised the dead. Many hailed him as the greatest prophet of his era, a man who routinely performed miracles and who transformed lives through his inspired teaching and the irresistible power of his formidable personality.

His name was Apollonius of Tyana, and, for the first few centuries of the Christian era, he was more famous than Jesus Christ.

The Roman emperors Nerva and Titus sought Apollonius' blessings before beginning their rule. Both Nero and Domitian, stung by Apollonius' denunciations of their bloody reigns, unsuccessfully attempted to have him executed.

After his death near the age of one hundred, Apollonius' legend continued to grow. In the early third century, Emperor Caraculla traveled to Tyana to pray at the site where Apollonius had first become known as a leading physician of his day. A few years later Emperor Alexander Severus erected statues in his private chapel of the men he considered the greatest figures of antiquity—Alexander the Great, Orpheus, Abraham, Jesus Christ, and Apollonius of Tyana. Emperor Hadrian collected letters from Apollonius and preserved them in his personal library in Antium.

In 271 C.E., Lucius Aurelian led an army against Tyana, the city in Cappadocia (in today's eastern Turkey) where Apollonius had been born nearly three centuries earlier. When the citizens resisted, Aurelian swore he would not leave even a dog alive. Roman historians claim that Apollonius materialized in front of the emperor in his tent, commanding him to show mercy. Aurelian instantly stopped the assault and built a shrine to Apollonius at the site.

Apollonius was not only honored (or feared) by the upper echelons of Roman society. He was also embraced by the common people, who built memorials to him throughout West Asia, where he was remembered as a healer with powers of nearly mythical proportions. His medical skills saved thousands from plague and pestilence.

Apollonius is one of the Greek-speaking spiritual teachers known to have visited India. Almost miraculously, records of the period he spent living with a community of yogis in the Himalayan foothills have survived to the present day. We know that he wrote a four-volume work describing the teachings he received from the yogis, and that he spent the next sixty years of his life traveling throughout Persia, Greece, Rome, Spain, North Africa, and Egypt, calling for reform of religion and society along the Indian model and relating his experiences with the yogis, whom he called "gods among men."

So much information about Apollonius' life has survived

thanks to a Syrian disciple named Damis. Damis joined the master on his trek to India and kept a diary detailing Apollonius' adventures for the rest of the sage's life. In the middle of the third century Julia Domna—empress of Rome and an admirer of Apollonius—acquired the diary and passed it on to Flavius Philostratus, one of the major literary figures of the day. She asked him to prepare a biography of the master, a task that Philostratus completed with relish. He visited communities where Apollonius was particularly well remembered to collect stories about him passed down through the generations, and referred to Apollonius' own voluminous writings, as well as numerous books about the master composed by other authors. Philostratus' retelling of Apollonius' amazing life is still available today.

Born to a wealthy Tyanian family, Apollonius showed little interest in the self-indulgent upper-class lifestyle available to him. We know that as a young man he studied in Tarsus under a Phoenician tutor, but his attraction to healing and mysticism soon drew him to the temple of Asclepius in the town of Aegae. Asclepius was the Greek god of medicine whose temples served as hospitals and "outpatient clinics" in the Hellenistic period. Absorbing the medical wisdom of his day, Apollonius matured into an adept physician. Cultivating the vigorous health that would sustain him through nearly a century of constant travel, he gave up meat and alcohol, preferring fresh vegetarian foods and clean water. Though he inherited a great deal of money he gave most of it away, preferring a simple lifestyle devoted to teaching and service.

Yet an unfulfilled desire burned in a well-lit corner of Apollonius' soul. He dreamed of visiting the sages of India.

It's important to understand that Apollonius of Tyana was a devout follower of Pythagoras and may well have been aware of the tradition that Pythagoras studied with Indian masters.

Apollonius adopted the Pythagorean dress code (similar to that of many yogis: long hair and beard, no clothing made from slaughtered animals) and code of conduct, but the five-year period of silence (Sanskrit, *mauna*) all Pythagoreans were required to undergo was a difficult test. Passing through the town of Aspendus, he found a mob preparing a pyre to burn their governor alive. "Two rich businessmen bought up all the grain and are keeping it in storage, hoping to make a huge profit. In the meantime, the people are starving!" the terrified governor explained. "It was a legal sale so there's nothing I can do."

Apollonius climbed onto a platform before the mob and—determined not to break his vow of silence even in this emergency—signaled to the townspeople to calm down. Something about his demeanor affected everyone present and incredibly, the rioting stopped. Apollonius directed the townspeople to fetch the two businessmen, but without harming them. When they were brought forward, he handed them a written message: "Our mother the Earth provides for all of us because she is just. Because you are unjust you have hoarded her gifts, as if she were your mother alone." The corn dealers experienced a quick change of heart and decided to give the grain away for free. (Given the murderous anger of the crowd, this was no doubt a prudent business decision.) Apollonius' ability to inspire crowds—in this case without uttering a single word—served him well years later when he returned from India, traveling from town to town teaching and healing.

Whether he had learned about the yogis from fellow Pythagoreans who believed Pythagoras had absorbed much of his knowledge from Indian brahmins centuries earlier, whether he was influenced by stories brought back from India by Alexander's armies, whether he heard of them from the *gymnosophists* (Indian ascetics) known to be teaching in Rome by the first century, or whether as a resident of Asia Minor he had heard rumors about the extraordinary wisdom and powers of the yogis from his Persian neighbors (at this time Persia controlled northwestern India), Apollonius was determined to reach the sages of the Himalayas.

## Himalayan Pilgrimage

With a hardy group of disciples, including Damis, who dutifully recorded the events of the journey, Apollonius traveled overland through Persia. There he paused for nearly two years in Babylon to visit the Magi, legendary Zoroastrian priests whose sacred language, Avestan, is a dialect of Sanskrit. He then pushed on through what is now Afghanistan, emerging through the Khyber Pass into the city of Taxila, at the northwestern tip of greater India.

As visitors from abroad, the party was soon ushered into the home of Phraotes, the local maharaja. Phraotes first interviewed them through an interpreter but then turned to Apollonius and said in perfect Greek, "You and I, I hope, will become good friends."

Apollonius was shocked. "You speak Greek? Why did you conceal this?"

"We have many foreign guests," Phraotes answered, "travelers who come to India hoping to partake of our fabled wealth. It is rare for one to come hoping to partake of our wisdom. I will help you find those you seek."

A few days later Apollonius and his small band were on their way into the Himalayan foothills, led by an experienced guide carrying a letter from Phraotes himself to Iarchas, guru of the mountain yogis. It said, "This Apollonius, a wise man, believes you are wiser than himself, and comes to learn your lore. Please send him away only when he knows what you know, for he will use the knowledge well."

The exact location that Apollonius was taken to is difficult to trace from Philostratus' account, but it appears to have been in northeastern Punjab, or perhaps Kashmir. As they neared a village, a young, dark-skinned boy came running to greet them calling, "You must come at once! The masters are asking for you." Following this new guide to the mountain ashram, the travelers caught their first glimpse of the community of yogis: barefoot, bearded men wearing simple cloth that Damis describes as being made from "wool growing on the earth" (Indian cotton). The yogis were chanting their midday hymn to the Sun, most likely the Gayatri mantra.

"At last you have arrived!" the guru Iarchas greeted the group. Apollonius began to introduce himself but Iarchas stopped him. "We are not so ignorant that we don't know who comes." Iarchas then revealed that he knew not only Apollonius' name but also his parents' names, the outline of his life history, and the details of his long journey.

The Greeks were astonished. "How can you possibly know these things?" Apollonius demanded.

"We begin," Iarchas explained, "by knowing ourselves."

Over the months that followed, Apollonius received intensive yogic training, involving both a thorough grounding in yoga philosophy and its practical application in yoga practice. He was introduced to the Vedic method of performing *pujas* (sacred rituals), and to secret aspects of yogic science such as the Vedic system of astrology and techniques of controlling matter through the manipulation of sunlight *(surya vidya)*. He learned to work with mantras and how to empower yantras. (For centuries after his death, European historians record, the sacred yantras created by Apollonius were treasured throughout Western Asia). But most of all, he learned to know himself. Iarchas taught that when the mind is purified, the divine knowledge at the root of our being is revealed, and we locate our own Higher Self in the Self of all.

Damis did not always understand the finer points of Indian philosophy and was not allowed to be present during some aspects of the yogic training. He did note down the more sensational events he witnessed, such as yogis discussing their previous lives as casually as if they were describing what they'd eaten for dinner the evening before. One day he even thought he saw a yogi levitating. He was also impressed by the enormous respect the Indian people had for the sages and described how the yogis compassionately but firmly advised kings and other statesmen who came to them for guidance.

Damis included one rather amusing story of an event that occurred early during their stay. Several boy-yogis invited Apollonius to tell them about the men Greeks admired most. Apollonius spoke passionately about the great Greek heroes of the Trojan War, whose adventures were chronicled by the ancient poet Homer. When he finally finished, he was surprised that rather than responding appreciatively, the boys sat in stunned silence. "You mean," one of them finally ventured, "in your country people honor *warriors* instead of *saints*?"

When at last it was time to depart, Apollonius left a note for Iarchas and the other sages. Damis kept a copy: "I came to you on foot, and you poured into me wide vistas of knowledge that allow my spirit to soar. When I return to the West I'll testify to the entire world of your wisdom. I will honor you till my last breath."

Philostratus records many stories, well known at the time, of Apollonius' deeds when he reached home. Once he stopped a funeral procession and raised a young girl "from the dead." This gave rise to rumors that he was a sorcerer with power over death, even though he himself explained over and over that as a physician, he was able to recognize that the girl had been in a coma and he had merely used his medical skills to revive her. (In a remarkably similar incident when Jesus "raised" the daughter of a local ruler, he too explained that the girl "had only been sleeping.")

One of the most famous stories came from Ephesus, a city where Apollonius was particularly beloved. He spent months there preaching and healing, as usual emphasizing in his public talks the importance of high moral standards, while reserving deeper aspects of spiritual training for the more serious disciples who came to him. Before leaving the city, however, he upbraided the people for the poor levels of sanitation they tolerated and warned that an epidemic would inevitably result. Several months after he left, plague broke out, and a delegation of desperate citizens was sent to beg him to return. Apollonius' heroic efforts to save the Ephesians from the plague were commemorated with a statue of the master that stood in Ephesus for generations.

But Apollonius' most important work was probably that which the public didn't see. Hellenistic religion had degenerated to the point that many of the priests and priestesses in Greek and Roman temples were merely going through the motions of spiritual life, having forgotten the real significance of their rituals. Even great spiritual centers were rapidly deteriorating into businesses run by corrupt priests. We are told that at every city he visited, these temples were Apollonius' first concern. He was usually greeted warmly because of his reputation as an accomplished master and would sit down with the priests, telling them, "I have beheld men dwelling on Earth yet not of it, who were fortified without fortifications, who owned nothing and yet possessed everything." He would tell them of India, rekindle their enthusiasm for spiritual practice, and explain the true significance of their religious myths, as his guru Iarchas had clarified for him years earlier.

In this era, Egypt was the most spiritually oriented civilization well known to the West. Apollonius decided to visit Egypt in order to compare its wisdom with that of India's yogic tradition. He spent years in Egypt and made the long journey up the Nile to visit the Ethiopian ascetics who sought spiritual truths in the desert. According to Philostratus, Apollonius was distressed by what he found in Egypt: this great spiritual tradition was also in decline. Apollonius found evidence that some "Ethiopians" had emigrated from India in remote antiquity but had been cut off from their original gurus in India for so long, they had gradually lost much of their original spiritual vitality. Oddly, classical authors sometimes confused India with Ethiopia. If Apollonius was correct that teachers from India settled in northeastern Africa in antiquity, this would no longer be so surprising. It is certainly curious that the Egyptian names for the deities Osiris and Isis—Asar and Isis—are so similar to very ancient Sanskrit words for *god* and *goddess*—Asura and Ishi. There is also a tradition preserved by the Greeks that Osiris visited India in remote antiquity—another curious link between the ancient Hindu and Egyptian cultures.

Sadly, by the first century C.E., the level of spiritual life at the Egyptian temples was deplorable. Apollonius was upset to find that the conservative priesthood had become lazy and arrogant. Not surprisingly, the Egyptians were irritated by the Greek upstart who insisted their temples needed reforming. "Who has the authority to teach Egyptian priests their own religion?" one hierophant angrily demanded.

"Anyone," Apollonius calmly replied, "who comes from India."

## Erasing History

Near the end of his life, when Apollonius was called to Rome to answer charges of sorcery instigated by his bitter enemy, the brutal emperor Domitian, the Greek sage explained that he was not practicing magic but the sciences of India. Having traveled most of the world known to the Greeks, having studied with the fabled Magi of Persia and the priests and ascetics of Egypt, Apollonius frankly stated that he had never found such wisdom anywhere in the world as he had discovered among the Indians. He went so far as to claim that many of the mystery schools of the West had originated in India in the distant past. Apollonius was exonerated of all charges and released.

One day, probably in his nineties, Apollonius simply walked out the door and was never seen again. No one knows exactly where and when he died. His memory was lovingly preserved for centuries in the eastern portion of the empire, where much of his healing and teaching work had been focused, and also, surprisingly, among the Arabs. In fact, Apollonius remains to this day an important figure in Islamic esotericism.

But few of us in the West have ever heard of Apollonius, much less of his connection with the yogic tradition. Why is this? Early in the fourth century a Roman governor named Hierocles was so impolitic as to remark to Church authorities that there have been saints in all spiritual traditions, not only in Christianity, and that some of them, like Apollonius of Tyana, were known to have performed miracles similar to those of Christ. Instantly, the full brunt of Christian orthodoxy was brought to bear against the memory of Apollonius. In 331 Constantine the Great sent a contingent of troops to Aegae; the temple of Asclepius where Apollonius had first practiced medicine was smashed to pieces. In Ephesus, the statue of Apollonius was toppled and buried. All of Apollonius' writings, including his multivolume work on the teachings of the yogis, were tracked down and burned. Numerous shrines to Apollonius (including several built by earlier Roman emperors), as well as copies of every book written about him, were destroyed. A few copies of Philostratus' biography, some pieces of correspondence preserved in private collections, and numerous references to Apollonius in the works of other authors of the time are all we have left of the sage of Tyana.

The following letter, probably written toward the close of the first century, is one of the few scraps of Apollonius' own writings that survives.

## Apollonius of Tyana to Governor Valerius, on the Death of His Son

No one ever dies, they only appear to, just as no one is actually born, though they appear to enter this world. When consciousness shifts from spirit into matter, we say a soul has come into existence, and when it shifts from matter to spirit, we say a soul has passed out of existence. In reality our divine essence is never born and is never destroyed. It is a mistake to claim that because a person can be seen by our eyes he exists, but when he can no longer be grasped by our physical senses he no longer exists.

People do not understand that although a child is brought into the world by its parents, he is not created by his parents. It is God alone who exists, taking on the names and forms of individual beings. Some people weep when God withdraws from a form back into his own eternal essence, although God has only changed his place, not his nature. Truly we should not lament another's death, but honor it. And the most perfect way to honor your son's passing is to release him to God, and continue to rule as you did before over the people entrusted to your care. That man is most fit to govern others who has first governed himself. You must master your grief.

What piety is there in weeping over events ordained

by God? If divine will is at the root of the world, and it is, then a just man will not despise God's blessings but accept that everything that happens, happens for the best. Go forward then and heal yourself, rule justly, and console the unfortunate. It is not your purpose on Earth to sit and weep but to wipe away the tears of others.

You are the governor of fifty cities and the noblest of Romans. If I could be with you, I would persuade you not to mourn.

Today Apollonius has been almost completely forgotten, a dim legend it's hard to believe ever even existed. Then a few years ago archaeologists excavating in Turkey stumbled across a stone, housed now in the Adana Museum. It was apparently originally part of an ancient shrine, long since smashed to bits, and was inscribed in Greek with these words:

> Apollonius was like the sun,
> shining forth from Tyana.
> He was sent by heaven
> to relieve our suffering.

# CHAPTER THIRTEEN

# The Priest of Delphi

## PLUTARCH

PLUTARCH WAS A PRIEST AT THE TEMPLE of Delphi, the spiritual center of the Greek world. More than a hundred of his essays have survived, offering us a fascinating glimpse into the religious, scientific, and political worlds of his era. His thoughtful and very readable books invite us directly into the mind of this well-educated and deeply spiritual man.

We know only a few facts about Plutarch's life, but what we do know is highly impressive. Born about 45 C.E. in central Greece, he studied at the Platonic Academy in Athens, then moved to Rome, where he distinguished himself as a scholar, statesman, teacher, and historian. Emperor Trajan eventually raised him to consular rank, one of the highest honors in the Roman Empire. He was appointed procurator by Emperor Hadrian in 119, another extraordinary honor. For more than twenty years he also served the god Apollo at Delphi, a position to which he brought kindness, dignity, and intellectual depth.

Today Plutarch is best remembered as the author of *Lives*, biographies of leading figures in Greece and Rome. Less well remembered is that he often wrote warmly in support of women. His essays include "The Bravery of Women" and "Sayings of the

Spartan Women," as well as a moving letter to his grief-stricken wife following the death of their two-year-old daughter. He also candidly shared his perspectives on religion, vegetarianism (humane treatment of animals was a hot topic then as now), and life after death. His insights are as valuable now as they were two thousand years ago.

## Understanding the Gods

Like many educated people of his day, Plutarch was well versed in the culture and philosophy of Egypt. This is particularly evident in his essay "Isis and Osiris," in which he lists some of the giants of Greek history who studied with Egyptian priests (Solon, Thales, Pythagoras, Plato, etc.). The essay is directed to one of Plutarch's peers, a priestess named Clea, who served the Egyptian goddess Isis. He begins by reminding her what it means to be a true votary of the divine.

"God isn't wonderful because he is fabulously wealthy, or because he's so powerful he can control the thunder and lightning. What makes him so great is his limitless knowledge and awareness. The purpose of our work as priests and priestesses is to attain knowledge of him, the first, the supreme ruler, the ideal one.

"The search for truth requires intense study and concentration. This quest is more holy than any other and is most pleasing to the goddess you worship. Indeed when Typhon, her enemy, rips the sacred texts to shreds, it is Isis who collects them together again, and entrusts them to those initiated in the holy mysteries."

Plutarch mentioned the famous statue of Isis at Sais in northern Egypt, which bears the inscription "I am all that was, all that is, and all that ever will be. No mortal has lifted my veil." But Plutarch intended to try. In an effort to understand who and what the Greek and Egyptian deities really were, he carefully considered seven theories about the nature of the gods. For those of us raised in Western monotheistic religions, his views provide a fascinating glimpse into polytheism, revealing how the ancients thought about their many gods and goddesses.

*Theory 1.* The gods were originally soldiers and kings whose legends were greatly exaggerated over time. The god Osiris and the demon Typhon were simply military commanders whose all-too-human conflict was still commemorated by the Egyptians. (Let me insert here that ancient India recognized an identical class of semidivine beings called Asura. In Scandinavia they were called Aesir, the Mesopotamians called them Assyr, and in Egypt the king of the demigods was named Asar, or Osiris in Greek. Many modern Western scholars believe the Sanskrit word *asura* originally meant a "lord" or military leader, echoing the theory mentioned by Plutarch here.) Plutarch was completely disgusted with this view, which he felt led to atheism.

*Theory 2.* Plutarch was happier with the hypothesis that such beings as Isis and Osiris may have been "heroes," superhuman individuals whose actual existence, he points out, was attested by numerous ancient historians. These heroes were more than human, but less than divine. Their accomplishments were superhuman, such as Osiris' legendary conquest and civilizing of much of the known world, as far as India. However, their personalities were still compromised by passion, so they could not be considered fully divine.

Plutarch theorized that some heroes, such as Isis and Osiris in Egypt, or Dionysus and Hercules in Greece, actually elevated themselves to the rank of gods through their extraordinarily courageous acts on behalf of their people.

*Theory 3.* Plutarch also considered the suggestion that the gods stood for natural phenomena. Osiris represented the Nile, for example, while his wife, Isis, symbolized the lush soil of Egypt, which is fertilized by the Nile. Typhon, their great enemy, stood for drought or for the desolate Egyptian desert beyond the reach of the Nile's life-giving waters. This was actually the interpretation of Egyptian mythology favored by many European scholars in the nineteenth and twentieth centuries, though Plutarch considered this an extremely superficial level of analysis.

Incidentally, it would be a mistake to dismiss the ancient Greeks' and Egyptians' level of geological sophistication. Plutarch pointed out that shells had been found all over Egypt, even in its mines and mountains, indicating that at one time the country was covered by a sea. Many springs and wells, he noted, contained brackish water, further evidence that northeastern Africa was once submerged in saltwater. Modern geologists have only recently confirmed this.

*Theory 4.* The gods clearly represent astronomical phenomena. Osiris, for example, can be equated with the Moon; he ruled for twenty-eight years, which corresponds to the Moon's cycle of twenty-eight days. His great enemy, Typhon, then symbolized the lunar eclipse. In Egyptian mythology, Isis doesn't kill Typhon, despite her son's angry objections. Plutarch pointed out that Isis could not destroy Typhon because the eclipse cycle will endure as long as the Sun and Moon continue to exist.

Plutarch also referenced the association between the Egyptian deities and particular stars and constellations. Isis was connected with Sirius, the brightest star in the sky. Plutarch identified her son Horus with the constellation the Greeks called Orion.

*Theory 5.* Next Plutarch investigated the psychological significance of the deities. Osiris represents everything that is good in us, the healthiest parts of our personality. When we are thinking and acting most clearly and benevolently, Osiris is at work in us. He represents our purest intuitions and well-reasoned actions. Typhon, on the other hand, is our irrational nature, the angry, impulsive, selfish, and unruly part of our psyche, which too often overshadows our better nature. We need look no further than the conflicts in our own psyche to find the battleground of the gods.

*Theory 6.* Plutarch then considered the idea that the gods are really cosmological principles. "Isis is the principle of nature, the living matter of the universe which aspires to union with Osiris, her transcendent lover. He exists far beyond material nature, for he never changes, decays, or dies. He is the supreme beauty, the ultimate good that nature longs to embrace." We ourselves cannot experience Osiris as long as we remain bound by our bodies and emotions, unless we cleanse and refine our minds and hearts through spiritual practice.

According to Plutarch, the meaning of the gruesome story of Osiris being dismembered by Typhon was that bits or "images" of Osiris' divine consciousness are impressed on matter, like seals impressing their images on melted wax. We see these impressions as the beauty and order of nature, which reveal the perfection of Osiris' higher awareness. But none of these impressions lasts; eventually they all dissolve in the swirling vortex of material substance. After death the purest and most dispassionate of us, Plutarch says, leave the realm of Isis and follow Osiris to an imperishable inner reality.

*Theory 7.* According to the last hypothesis, it's wrong to simply say the Sun or Earth or sky is Isis or Osiris, or that their adventures are just allegories for planting or plowing. "Rather, if we honor everything that is good and helpful and orderly as the work of Isis, being a reflection of the divine consciousness of Osiris, we will not be mistaken."

Plutarch concluded that one cannot say Isis and Osiris or the other Egyptian deities are gods of Egypt alone. "These gods belong to all people everywhere. From the beginning of time people throughout the world have acknowledged and worshiped the same divine powers. Just as the Sun and Moon and stars are common to all people, so the gods are common to all, even though different people call them by different names.

"The greatest lovers of wisdom observed the mysterious presence of the divine in all things, animate and inanimate. Like them, we should honor the intelligence that operates in nature. It is not that we should worship these natural forces as distinct gods and goddesses but as clearer mirrors of the divine itself, as living instruments of the one God who rules them all."

## Words of Wisdom from Gryllus the Pig

One of Plutarch's liveliest essays is called "Animals Are Rational." It's based on the episode in Homer's *Odyssey* in which our shipwrecked hero, Odysseus, takes refuge on the island of Circe the sorceress. Circe is attracted to Odysseus and keeps him around as her lover. His fellow sailors, however, she unceremoniously transforms into pigs.

In Plutarch's version, when Odysseus decides he's had enough of the sorceress's charms and wants to go home, he storms in to Circe and demands that she return his shipmates to their human form.

"I can't do that," she responds. "Even a magician as powerful as myself can't turn pigs into men against their will."

"My men are counting the minutes till they can return to Greece with me!" Odysseus retorts angrily.

"Oh yeah? See for yourself." Circe waves her hand and one of the pigs, formerly Odysseus' shipmate Gryllus, gains the power to speak fluent Greek.

"Get the men ready," Odysseus commands. "Circe's changing you back into sailors, and we're heading home."

"No way!" shouts Gryllus.

"You've got to be kidding! You guys want to be human again, don't you?"

"Not on your life! Odysseus, you're just like the little kid who runs away when the doctor comes to give him medicine, or who hides when it's time to go to school. Circe could have changed you into a pig too, in which case you'd be much wiser and healthier than you are now. You want us to give up the good life to sail away with you? Forget it!"

"Circe must have drugged you!"

"Hey, big brain, I won't stand for your insulting a noble lady! But instead of yelling at each other, let's discuss this situation rationally."

"Oh, this I've got to hear."

"We animals are vastly superior to you human beings, particularly in the area of ethics," Gryllus began. "Without even having been taught, we live far more moral lives."

"Give me a break! What kind of virtue is there in animals?"

"First there's courage. That's a virtue you've often laid claim to, Odysseus, not even having the grace to blush when you're hailed as the 'sacker of cities.' You coward, you won your Trojan War through lies and deceit! We animals fight honestly with true, valiant spirit. Even our women are courageous—in fact there's no force in nature more ferocious than one of our females defending her young. But look at your wife, Penelope—your house is overrun with vagrants and rather than lifting a finger to throw them out, she sits timidly year after year, waiting for you to come home and rescue her!

"If you humans are so much braver than us, why do your poets call your warriors 'lion-hearted' and 'bold as a boar,' but they never call one of us 'man-hearted' or 'bold as a boy'? Animals fight with their whole heart, but your hearts are divided by plots and fears and calculations. No wonder when danger arises your courage so often fails you. It's not nature's fault that it didn't give you tusks or claws or stings—you're just natural weaklings."

"Yeah? What about temperance, then? Pigs aren't exactly known for that virtue!"

"Odysseus, I've never heard of an animal wanting to have sex with a man, but I've heard plenty about the variety of creatures you men will use as long as they fit. So much for temperance!

"Temperance means curtailing superfluous desires and applying self-discipline in the fulfillment of our true needs. When I was human, I saw you in Crete decked out in a gorgeous woven tunic and a purple wool coat. How I envied you! I was absolutely sick with jealousy. Look at me now—all the gold and silver nuggets in the world don't tempt me more than any other rock.

"These days I'm completely content resting in a deep bank of soft mud! But you humans are never content. Even when you have everything you need, you actively invent more desires. We animals never take more than we need—but you humans never *stop* taking more than you need. Humans are the only creatures that seek out luxury.

"It doesn't matter how sick indulging yourselves makes you—you can't stop yourselves from pursuing every kind of pleasure. We animals have sensitive noses that tell us whether a food is good or bad for us and stop us from eating unhealthy things before the damage is done. We eat only the foods appropriate to our species, but you eat every delicacy you can stuff in your mouths—and then wail when you feel sick afterward!

"You need to be taught technology and the sciences, but we know them from birth. We know what herbs to eat when we're injured. Who taught beavers to build dams or birds to build nests?

"You feel you're superior because you pass your poetry and plays to future generations. We pass our arts to our children too.

Have you noticed that if you take a nestling away from its parents and raise it yourselves, it never learns to sing? This is because it left its teachers too early."

Odysseus was becoming increasingly flustered, but he had one arrow left in his quiver. "We humans are and always will be superior to animals! Only we have knowledge of God!"

Plutarch ends the essay slyly by making Gryllus, rather ungenerously, remind Odysseus about Odysseus' own father, Sisyphus, the most notorious atheist in the Greek world!

## The Flesh Eaters

If "Animals Are Rational" is Plutarch's most charming work, "The Eating of Flesh" is perhaps his most passionate. A committed vegetarian, Plutarch appealed with his readers to stop their inhumanity toward animals.

In this essay Plutarch asked how humans could ever have begun a practice as inherently revolting as eating flesh. "It must have been at some catastrophic point in history, when climatic forces destroyed the vegetation and our ancestors were reduced to desperate poverty. But those of you who are alive now, when there is more than enough fruit and grain and nuts to eat, what could possibly induce you to shed blood for the sake of your palates? It's a slander against your mother the Earth to act as if her grains and vegetables are not sufficient to feed you. You call lions and panthers savage, but they kill only to survive. You can easily thrive without slaughter, yet you kill anyway. Nor is it wolves or lions you destroy—animals that are genuinely dangerous—but the gentle, defenseless creatures nature designed for their beauty and grace.

"It's a horrible thing to see how the tables of the rich are laden with the dead bodies of innocents, and cooks hired to dress the dead! Then at the end of the feast large quantities of meat are thrown away—those animals died for no reason at all."

Plutarch argued powerfully that meat eating is contrary to human nature. He correctly pointed out that unlike carnivores, human hands and jaws are not designed for the capture of prey, nor are our digestive systems designed to process large quantities of meat. (Carnivores have very short intestinal tracts that can quickly expel the toxins present in raw meat. Humans have very long intestines, designed to slowly break down vegetable matter.)

Not only are human bodies not built for flesh eating, neither are our souls. Plutarch made the point that while a hungry man can visualize with great relish taking a fruit from a tree or a melon from a vine, there are very few of us who can cheerfully visualize capturing prey with our bare hands, ripping its still-living body open with our teeth, and starting to feed. For true carnivores, this should be an appealing fantasy. The only way most people can bring themselves to eat flesh at all is to cook it and dress it with spices, disguising its real nature from themselves.

Meat, Plutarch concluded, being an improper food for humans, is not only unhealthy for the body, it's also bad for the soul. After a vegetarian meal, a person feels light, refreshed, and clearheaded. After a meal of flesh, however, the body becomes agitated and lethargic. "The innate light of the soul becomes dim and confused, since its natural brilliance cannot radiate through a body that's gorged itself on flesh."

Plutarch admitted that convincing people to abandon a diet of meat is almost impossible "since bellies have no ears." Nevertheless, the casual attitude toward killing that meat eating induces contributes to the moral depravity of man, Plutarch insisted, as was evident in the gladiatorial arenas.

The greatest of the Greek sages, such as Pythagoras and Empedocles, were vegetarians. "These were the philosophers who tried to humanize us, who taught us to act justly not only toward each other but toward other creatures also."

Plutarch's argument is certainly as relevant today as it was two thousand years ago.

## The Vision of Aridaeus

For the student of spirituality today, perhaps the most valuable portions of Plutarch's voluminous works are his three myths: the myths of Aridaeus, of Timarchus, and of the Island of Cronus. Nowadays *myth* means a story that isn't literally true. However, in Plutarch's time a *mythos* simply meant a story that couldn't be verified. You believed—or disbelieved—it at your own risk.

Aridaeus made an enormous fortune the old-fashioned way: he cheated everyone he met. Plutarch remarks that Aridaeus "abstained from no evil action that led to wealth or pleasure." He sent a message to the Oracle at Cilicia to ask if he would do even better as he got older. The Oracle responded, "You will do better when you die."

As fate would have it, not long afterward Aridaeus fell from a height. The blow to his head killed him instantly. Three days later, as his funeral was concluding, Aridaeus suddenly sat up, and over the next few days regained his strength. But he was so dramatically changed his friends scarcely knew him. He was now the incarnation of integrity, generosity, and piety. Protogenes was with him when he finally related how he became so transformed, and it was Protogenes who relayed the mythos to Plutarch.

At the moment of his fall, Aridaeus felt himself being ejected from his body, then floating upward toward the stars. His field of vision broadened as if his soul were an eye able to see all around him at once.

As he rose higher he saw a number of other bubble-shaped

souls racing to and fro in the atmosphere. Some flitted forward in straight lines, others in spirals, and some suddenly shifted upward then abruptly shot back down. (Modern readers may be taken aback by how much the bubble-like souls streaking across the sky sound like UFO reports!)

Gradually the souls of the recently deceased assumed shapes similar to the physical body from which they had just been expelled. Some of the souls were racing around in blind panic, unable to help or be helped by others, while the calmer souls continued to rise higher, expressing their delight as they recognized each other.

A distant relative, long since deceased, appeared before Aridaeus. "You know, you're not really dead," the relative explained. "Part of your soul is still back in your body, like an anchor." Aridaeus now noticed a shadowlike cable trailing behind his subtle form, connecting him to his physical body far below. Greatly relieved, he collected his wits and asked his disembodied mentor what was going on.

"*Adrasteia* is the supreme ruler of the world," his relative explained. "Adrasteia is the law of reaping what we've sown—all of us are recompensed for our thoughts and actions during life, both the good and the evil. The lucky ones are those whose evils were exposed during their lifetimes, who paid their penalties while they were still alive and arrive here unburdened by those debts. Those who thought they could get away with their crimes, or who continued to cling to their vices, are punished here in the afterlife, where the pain of guilt and grief is a hundred times more intense than it is in the body. The very worst souls, the irredeemable ones, are carried off by the horrible goddess Erinys and are never seen again."

Aridaeus was amazed to note that you could actually tell the status of each soul's impurity by the color of the light that shimmered around it. Dirty-brown souls were heavy with greed and selfishness; blood-red souls blazed with anger and malevolence. Some of the souls were a silvery blue, signaling that much of their inner vice had been painfully cleansed away. And still others, incapable of releasing their desire for more pleasures of the body, were on their way back to Earth to be reborn in yet another physical body.

His guide carried him for what seemed like an incredible distance till they came to the most beautiful garden Aridaeus had ever seen. The souls there were joyous, and delight permeated the atmosphere like a fragrance. Aridaeus wanted to stay, but his relative warned him sternly, "You must not stop in this terrible place. Here good-hearted souls experience every pleasure, being rewarded for their good deeds on Earth. While they linger they forget the purpose of their journey, and the innermost part of their intelligence wastes away. All too soon they'll be forced to return to Earth, having thrown aside the opportunity to rise higher."

Further on they came to an enormous vortex in which all kinds of thoughts and memories were swirling. "This place is the source of dreams," the guide explained. "I had wanted to take you to see the source of Apollo's Oracle at Delphi, hidden here in the inner worlds, but I don't think your cable can extend that far." Aridaeus looked on ahead, but the light of the Oracle was so intense his eyes couldn't adjust. Still he caught snatches of the future being foreseen there: earthquakes and the fall of emperors and the time of his own death.

On their return they passed the place of torment, where criminals were brutally punished and hypocrites, who had always concealed their vicious passions, found the fantasies inside their minds projected outward for everyone to see. Aridaeus was horrified to find his father here. The man had secretly killed several of his guests and stolen their money. Here he was suffering so excruciatingly, Aridaeus couldn't bear to look. There was absolutely nothing he could do to help; his father had to suffer for his crimes. Aridaeus also saw souls who had despised each other so intensely in life that they now were wrapped around each other like snakes, literally eating each other alive.

Suddenly an incredibly voluptuous woman ran her fingers down Aridaeus' back, beckoning him to follow. Then he noticed she was holding a fiery spike in her hand with which she intended to impale him. In the sheer terror of that moment he collapsed back into his body, and opened his eyes just as his friends were about to lay him in his grave.

Plutarch included this story in his essay "The Delays of Divine Punishment."

## The Descent of Timarchus

Plutarch's essay "Socrates' Inner Guide" contains another myth, the tale of Timarchus, an equally fascinating account of a young spiritual aspirant who traveled to the Oracle of Trophonius, a site notorious for generating genuine spiritual visions, but at the cost of one's sanity, if not one's life. Timarchus descended into its underground crypt, where he lay in total darkness, awaiting a vision. Eventually he felt himself lifted into the heavens, where an unseen entity asked him, "Timarchus, what do you wish to know?"

"Everything!" Timarchus responded. "For what is there that isn't wonderful?"

The entity's teaching, as it was eventually transmitted to Plutarch, offers fascinating glimpses of the inner mysteries. It mapped the stages of the after-death experience in terms virtually identical to those of the sages of India.

Here is the description of the process of reincarnation. "Different entities enter their bodies to different degrees. Some lose themselves entirely in the body and are constantly distracted by their passions. Others merge in it only partially, the purest part of them remaining above the body like a buoy floating above the ocean. This portion is never overcome by the whims and desires of the physical body. The part submerged in the body is called the mind (*psyche* in Greek), but that part which remains above is the Higher Self (the *nous*)."

After he'd experienced numerous revelations in the crypt, Timarchus emerged radiant with inner light and shared his discoveries with friends. He died three months after his visit to Trophonius. (In Greek the words for "to be initiated" and "to die" are almost identical.) His friends eventually passed the story on to Plato's teacher, Socrates, says Plutarch. Plutarch believed this mythos offered an important clue to Socrates' legendary intuitive powers. Because of the purity and focus of his mind, Socrates was closely aligned with the part of his consciousness that remained above the body. This "oversoul" or "guardian angel" would provide guidance and extraordinary inspiration throughout his life.

In one of the most interesting passages in the essay, Plutarch explained that certain souls become so pure they no longer need to reincarnate. Yet some of them choose to remain near the Earth anyway. Just like coaches who help encourage young athletes, these special disembodied beings aid us here below "in the attainment of virtue and in the achievement of divine knowledge." This remarkable description correlates with the *gurudevas* and bodhisattvas of the Hindu and Buddhist traditions.

## The Isle of Cronos

"The Face on the Moon," one of Plutarch's most famous writings, contains another amazing parallel with Eastern traditions. "Many wrongly assume the Higher Self is somehow part of the mind, but that's as mistaken as supposing the mind is part of the body. Just as the mind is greater and more refined than the physical body, so the Higher Self is greater and more refined than the mind. The conjunction of mind and body produces reactions and emotions, which in turn generate pleasure and pain. The conjunction of the mind and Higher Self, however, create reason and intuitive insight, the use or misuse of which leads to virtue or vice.

"Our physical death reduces us to two factors, mind and Higher Self, out of three. Our second death reduces us from two factors to one, the Higher Self. The ultimate state is achieved when, sooner or later, the Self separates from the mind. Then the cast-off mind disintegrates in the mental world just as the cast-off body decays in the physical world. This separation occurs through the Higher Self's love for the inner sun, the supreme light which is the most beautiful, most divine and blessed state toward which all of nature in its own way aspires."

This is a remarkable description of the three bodies recognized in the yoga tradition, the *sthula upadhi, sukshma upadhi,* and *karana upadhi* or gross, subtle, and causal bodies. In *bindu bhedana,* one of the most esoteric yogic practices, the Higher Self enters the blazing light of the Inner Sun, called Savitar in Sanskrit, and passes out of this world system into the liberated state. Plutarch's detailed description of the process is proof that the Greeks were also aware of these advanced yogic states.

"The Face on the Moon" contains another huge surprise. In the myth of the Isle of Cronus detailed there, Plutarch mentioned that if you sail north to Britain, then continue west, you'll pass a series of islands (Iceland and Greenland). Eventually you'll reach "the great mainland," a huge land mass surrounded by an ocean. It's difficult to get to that continent, he warned, because of the "density of the sea [icebergs]."

Nearly fifteen hundred years before Columbus, Plutarch was describing North America.

# CHAPTER FOURTEEN

# From the Alone to the Alone

## PLOTINUS

IN HIS LATE THIRTIES, PLOTINUS set off on the long and danger-ous trek to India. Perhaps he'd been inspired by Apollonius of Tyana, whose books he may have read. By the third century C.E., the wisdom of the Himalayan masters had long been legendary in the Roman world. No doubt many Europeans dreamed of head-ing east to find a guru, then as now. But Plotinus could hardly have imagined, as he packed his bags for the journey, that within a few years some of the most illustrious men and women of Rome would be coming to *him* for spiritual guidance.

Plotinus was born in Egypt eighteen hundred years ago. We know little about his early life, but his biographer Porphyry does tell us that at the age of twenty-seven (around 231 C.E.), Plotinus met his master. He'd been living in Alexandria in Egypt, the intel-lectual center of the Roman Empire, for some time, but none of the teachers he studied with satisfied his yearning for direct experience of higher states of consciousness—till he met Ammonius Saccas.

Ammonius is one of the most mysterious figures in the history of Western spirituality, in part because (according to Porphyry) he made his disciples swear to strict secrecy. It's worth noting that Ammonius' two most famous students, Origen (possibly the

Christian remembered today as by far the most mystical of the Church Fathers) and Plotinus, both passed on teachings astonishingly close to those of the yogis of India. Perhaps it was Ammonius who encouraged Plotinus to seek out the Himalayan sages.

Determined to reach India, in 244 C.E. Plotinus joined the expedition of Emperor Gordion III traveling east into Persia. Rome suffered from a massive trade deficit to India owing to the insatiable desire of the Italians for quality Indian products. For centuries Roman armies marched eastward, attempting to punch a corridor through Persia in hopes of delivering more of their own goods to India in order to bolster the sagging Roman economy. Spiritual advisors such as Plotinus traveled with these armies in much the same capacity as chaplains accompany the military today. Plotinus hoped to get as far east as possible with the troops before heading out on his own through dangerous Persian territory into India. The trip was a disaster—the emperor was killed, and Plotinus barely managed to get back to Rome alive.

While he was no doubt disappointed not to lose himself in the Himalayas, it was extraordinarily fortunate for the Western world that Plotinus found himself instead in Rome, where he started a small school and began teaching a type of spirituality scholars today call Neoplatonism. It was rooted in the insights of Plato but enlivened by the brilliant mysticism of Ammonius. Though he didn't realize it, Plotinus was setting in motion a spiritual revolution.

Word quickly spread that a teacher who was not only brilliant (there was no shortage of highly intelligent men in Rome) but also genuinely saintly had arrived in town. Eventually Plotinus' students included not only other famous philosophers such as Porphyry (known as an astronomer and an early champion of animal rights) but also members of the Roman Senate and even

Caesar Gallienus himself, emperor of Rome from 253 to 268 C.E. Many notable women, among them Empress Cornelia Salonina, also studied with Plotinus.

Plotinus' reputation for wisdom, impeccable integrity, and true kindness made him a favorite counselor; contemporaries said it was extraordinary the way he could settle the most bitter disputes without making enemies. Because of his gentle nature and incorruptible moral core, parents with terminal diseases felt confident bringing their young children to him to raise, trusting the orphans would be safe and well educated in his care. Porphyry describes Plotinus—one of the greatest minds in the history of Western civilization—listening fondly as his little wards recited their multiplication tables over and over. Plotinus himself evidently never married, preferring a more ascetic lifestyle, and was a committed vegetarian, refusing even medicine if it contained animal products.

Once Plotinus happened to attend a lecture by a speaker named Diophanes. Diophanes claimed that if a spiritual teacher wanted to have sex with his disciple, it behooved the student to submit. Plotinus was so disgusted he got up several times to leave, but out of courtesy forced himself to sit through the talk. Afterward he asked Porphyry to write a refutation explaining why this type of behavior is entirely inappropriate and had him read the statement to his community of students.

Plotinus suffered from poor health much of his life, and his eyesight was so bad he never reread any of the essays he'd written. His concentration, however, was phenomenal. Porphyry reports the master could carry on an abstruse philosophical conversation while simultaneously writing a detailed analysis on an entirely different topic.

Today we think of philosophers as people who sit around

rationalizing about the nature of reality and writing incomprehensible books. Plotinus' attitude to philosophy, however, was entirely Eastern: he didn't just talk about the nature of things, he set about actively exploring different states of consciousness to test what insights each of them could offer. Plotinus was what the yogis call a *jnani*—a sage who achieves the highest mystical awareness through contemplation of the Inner Self. His doctrines about the Supreme Reality, the soul, and the universe emerged from his experiences in what the yogis call *samadhi*, states of intense meditative absorption. Porphyry reports that he himself watched Plotinus go into samadhi on four occasions.

Plotinus' influence on the Western world was immense. His ideas profoundly influenced the development of Christianity, largely through the work of the African Church Father Augustine. Augustine considered Plotinus a sort of reincarnation of Plato, the premier thinker of the Western tradition. When rabbis in medieval France discovered Plotinus' doctrines, they blended them into Jewish mysticism, reshaping Kabbalah into the form we know today. Marsilio Ficino helped spark the Renaissance in Europe in part through his translations of Plotinus' mind-expanding essays.

## Three Roads to Reality

What, then, was Plotinus teaching? We can understand reality on three different levels, he explained: transcendent Spirit, Cosmic Mind, and individual soul.

We are composite beings who exist simultaneously at all three levels of reality. We are aware of ourselves as individuals in the physical world. We're also aware of the mental universe when we turn our attention inward toward the archetypal patterns that shape our world. Plunging even deeper, we experience ourselves as a perfect unity that exists everywhere throughout all time and space at once. The difference between a drunk in the gutter, a physicist scribbling equations on a blackboard, and a mystic experiencing cosmic consciousness depends on which level each of them habitually focuses his awareness. We have a choice of worlds.

Plotinus stated the soul is, in a sense, "amphibious," living sometimes "here" in the deep and turbulent waters of material existence, and other times "there" in a tranquil realm of light. "The chains of our senses keep us bound here, as if we're trapped in a cave. However, deep within, the soul remembers its true nature. This recollection motivates it to begin meditating." This haunting remembrance of one's real nature is called *anamnesis* in Greek and *pratyabhijna* in Sanskrit.

Plotinus described a number of paths by which the soul can return to full awareness of the One. The first path is that of the lover. This personality type is obsessively drawn to a person who appears physically attractive. He must be taught that the beauty perceived in another person's body is only a dim reflection of pure spiritual beauty. This is why our inner sense of what beauty itself actually *is* never changes, even though outer beauty always fades away. "Lovers must be shown that there is beauty not only in physical bodies but in the arts and the sciences and in ethical values. This redirects their attention to the inner world, and from there they can begin the ascent to pure being, which is the supreme beauty." In India also the proper approach to beauty and desire is taught in some forms of spiritual practice. In the tradition of Sri Vidya, for example, divine reality itself is defined as *tripura sundari*, "the Supreme Beauty."

Second is the path of the artist, the person attracted to beauty not just in another human being but everywhere. "The artist and musician must be taught that the aesthetic qualities which so appeal to them actually come from within. They can then redirect their attention to the source of all beauty and harmony." Many musicians have commented that they didn't laboriously work out a song or a symphony—it simply appeared in their minds already complete, as if it were a gift from a higher realm. Plotinus believed that all great art comes from the inner world. In the Indian tradition also, musicians use their music as a form of spiritual practice, focusing on the *nada*, or inner sound, to lead them to its source in a higher world, much like meditators focus on their mantras.

The third path of philosophy is for more advanced souls "who have already turned their focus from the outer world toward the greater realities of the inner world but need someone to guide them further to the state of true freedom." Mathematics is a tool that Plotinus suggested philosophically oriented people can use to help them learn one-pointed concentration on nonmaterial realities. In India—regarded as the birthplace of mathematics by the Arabs—mathematical principles were coded into rituals and chants more than five thousand years ago. The altars and fire pits where Hindus performed their worship were constructed according to strict mathematical principles.

For Plotinus all three paths culminated in the practice of *dialektik* (Sanskrit *vichara*), meaning discriminating wisdom. "One learns to reason in a logical way, distinguishing between the real and the unreal, the truly worthwhile and the less valuable, the eternal and the noneternal. One's attention stops wandering in the outer universe and settles calmly in the inner world, where it divests itself of all forms of falsehood. Having wandered far, examining the whole structure of the universe, the soul returns to its starting point, leaving all thought behind, and releases itself into silence—for the enlightened state is perfectly still." In that state, as Plotinus described in detail, the thinker, the object of thought, and the thinking process itself all merge into One. "Here at last the soul arrives at transcendent unity."

## Meditation in Neoplatonism

In the *Enneads*, Plotinus recorded one of the meditations he taught his students. "Let us imagine the entire visible universe, holding it as clearly and distinctly in our mind as we are able. Visualize the Sun, the stars, and all living beings dwelling on the Earth or the sea. Watch them tranquilly, as if the entire cosmos existed inside a transparent sphere. Now call to mind the God who created this universe. Ask him to come bringing with him all the divine forces that exist within him. See that he and his creative energies and all the things he has created are not separate; they all exist together in perfect beauty. Imagine his limitless power extending to all infinity.

"You have been holding this image as if it were outside you. Now bring the vision inside yourself, as if *you* are that all-pervading God who holds all the universe within himself. Then dismiss the visual part of the meditation, and focus only on the living reality of God, the divine being who is silently present. Don't allow any sense of separateness to enter your awareness, but immerse yourself totally in the divine presence. If your attention shifts away, quickly bring it back to that feeling of divine unity.

"Surrender yourself completely to God, who at this very moment *is* holding you in his perfect, unitary awareness. If you imagine you're different from him, you are not yet in the fully illumined state. When you and he are perfectly one, with no sense of even the possibility that you could be two, then you have attained real understanding and true perception of your Highest Self, the Self that never departs from itself."

Yoga students will note how brilliantly Plotinus was leading his disciples from *savikalpa samadhi*, or unbroken meditation focused on a thought or image, into *nirvikalpa samadhi*, unbroken meditation on a higher reality beyond words and forms. Just like many yogis, he used a *mandala* or spherical mental object as the point of departure for his meditation.

## How God Does Everything

Also exactly like the Himalayan sages, Plotinus sometimes described the One as if it were a loving personal God, and at other times he spoke of it as totally impersonal, beyond any qualities whatsoever. In India the Supreme Reality is said to be *saguna*, to have qualities such as perfect love, wisdom, and power. At the same time it is said to be *nirguna*, to have no characteristics at all because in the One all qualities melt together into pure, undifferentiated consciousness. This might appear to be a contradiction to the logical mind, but the mystic experiences both in different stages of samadhi.

For most of us in the West, *God* means the Creator who made the heavens and Earth. For followers of Plato like Plotinus, the Creator or Cosmic Mind is not the highest reality. How then did Plotinus experience God, and where did the Cosmic Mind come from?

Plotinus taught that there is one Supreme Reality. This "One" is so wonderful that our limited minds can't even begin to imagine what it's like. It doesn't create the universe—in fact, it doesn't do anything at all. It's beyond time and space, action and nonaction, even beyond being itself. And yet everything comes from it.

This One brims with beauty and goodness, so much so that it "spills over" with its own perfection. Divine intelligence "pours" from it. Think of it this way. If you're a meditator you may occasionally experience a profound sense of inner stillness in which there's no thought, no sense of time passing or of space around you or inside you. There's no content in your awareness at all. In a sense "you" aren't there, and yet at the same time you are never more fully your true Self. Although "nothing" is there, a living presence—the light of your soul—is shining lucidly. Think of this as the transcendent One.

What happens next in your meditation? At some point, completely spontaneously, from out of the depths of this perfect stillness, thoughts simply start to "happen." Suddenly "you" are present not just as pure awareness but as a thinking entity. Similarly, in the One a Cosmic Mind spontaneously appears that "thinks" into being the seed patterns or archetypes around which the material world crystallizes. This "mind" is an inherent power of pure awareness.

In India many yogis held nearly identical beliefs. There the transcendent reality was called Brahman. The Cosmic Mind was called Brahma the Creator, or Hiranya Garbha, literally the "radiant womb" of consciousness. And the Supreme Reality as you experience it inside yourself during deep meditation is called Atman, the Self. This little Self is no different from the One than a drop of water is from the ocean, or the air in the eye of a tornado from the air outside the storm.

In the tradition of the Shaivite yogis, which developed in the foothills of the Himalayas, the One is called Shiva, who is simply *prakasha* (Sanskrit for "awareness" or "light of consciousness"). Shiva's innate ability to project universes "within" himself (just as we spontaneously create fantasy worlds when we dream, worlds that don't exist "outside" of ourselves) is called Shakti or *vimarsha* ("Self-awareness" or the "energy of consciousness"). There are numerous remarkable parallels between Plotinus and northern Shaivism.

As noted, the Cosmic Mind doesn't create the world in the sense that an architect sits down and carefully develops a blueprint, assembling workers and resources, and then directing the building process step-by-step. It simply calls them forth through the pure power of consciousness, just as we effortlessly call up the image of a house in our minds without having to think out every detail. Most of the objects we dream up are directly or indirectly based on objects we've seen earlier in the physical world. The Supreme Being's creative potency is so limitless, however, that it manifests infinite forms without needing any external model to inspire it.

The transcendent One doesn't think at all. There is nothing other than itself to think about, and no future or past in which evolution can occur. Rather, simply because it is, it constantly spontaneously emanates world systems, starting with the inner worlds of conscious creative energy. As their vibrations radiate further away from the One, these living patterns slip into time and causality. Finally matter appears, which Plotinus defines as "the furthest consciousness can travel from itself."

The One exists beyond space and time, so there is no question of a beginning or an end to the process of creative emanation. It occurs only now, which from our time-bound human standpoint means it occurs throughout all eternity.

## Radical Unity

The radical unity of all existence was one of Plotinus' favorite topics. "All things are joined together. The cosmos is a single complex creature, one living being made up of all living beings. Each member of the whole does its own work but also cooperates with every other member, for no one member is cut off from the whole." Saints are such remarkable people because they've surrendered their individual selfhood to the Self of all, and therefore they no longer act only on their own behalf; the whole of reality acts through them.

For Plotinus, the unity of existence and the timelessness of the Supreme Reality had startling consequences. Unlike orthodox scientists today who dismiss the "occult" sciences without pausing to test their validity, Plotinus was well acquainted with many forms of divination used in his day, from astrology to oracles like the one at Delphi, to augers who foretold the future from the flight of birds—and he admitted they could provide surprisingly accurate predictions. "Because the stars are interlinked with all things, they are able to signify everything that happens in the world we perceive." But how is this possible?

"Those who know how to read this kind of writing, as if the planets were letters in the sky, can determine the future from the patterns the planets form. But cause and effect aren't involved. The significance of the stars' message is found through analogy, just as the flight of birds doesn't *cause* men to follow a particular course of action but instead symbolically *reflects* what men choose to do."

Plotinus believed that by studying one part of the whole, you can learn about another. An Indian or Chinese doctor can diagnose a medical problem in your lungs by feeling the pulse in your wrist, for example. Or to borrow Plotinus' own example, you can tell a great deal about a person's mental state by looking at his eyes. "All things are filled with signs, and it is a wise person who can learn about one thing from another."

As you just learned, Plotinus believed the universe exists within the Cosmic Mind of the One. So at the root of the cosmos lies an infinite, unified intelligence. Because of this, *meaning* is inherent in all things. Skilled astrologers and augers can read the meaning spelled out all around us. Plotinus would never agree with modern scientists that the universe acts randomly and is purposeless. He found evidence of its inherent intelligence everywhere he looked.

## The Reincarnating Soul

Like the yogis, Plotinus taught that karma and reincarnation are the forces driving human existence. "Our character is related to the kind of person we were in our previous lives. If we want to understand ourselves fully, we have to take into account the moral choices we made in our past lives, because events happening to us now follow from them." He praised the "true justice and wonderful wisdom" of karma, called *adrasteia* in Greek, which literally means "inescapable." He also warned that those of us who cultivate animal-like habits in this life are in danger of being reborn as animals in the next life, while those of us who continually attune ourselves to nobler values may reincarnate in far more refined worlds than this one.

However, not rebirth in heavenly realms but freedom from the karmic process was the real goal for Plotinus, as it was for the saints and sages of India. While the rest of us are driven by our karma, which plays out in our lives as fate, Plotinus explained, "The man who lives a life of Self-awareness is his own driver and skillfully finds his own way."

Because karma and reincarnation are real principles playing out in our lives, the moral choices we make now are of critical importance. Plotinus offered the example of men who brutalize their slaves. These men will be reborn as slaves themselves in a future existence, he warned.

Plotinus' understanding of influences working in our lives was multidimensional: he acknowledged the impact of heredity, the environment, and even chance in creating the person we are today. But ultimately the responsibility for our lives lies with ourselves—we create our own reality, shaping our future through our attitudes and actions. "It is perhaps correct to say that when the soul acts unthinkingly, it is acting according to its destiny, but good and wise men act nobly and according to their own will. The best actions come from our own wise choices."

In the years I spent studying with the yogis and yoginis of India, one point was emphasized again and again: that freedom from the bondage of karma is possible only when instead of being controlled by habits and compulsions originating in the past, we learn to live with Self-awareness. Plotinus understood this perfectly and urged his disciples to honor the external universe but at the same time to explore the universe within, where the divine is more perfectly expressed. "There is a higher part of our soul which exists beyond the needs and preoccupations of the body, which belongs to the higher world. By turning toward this greater reality one comes to live freely and consciously, and becomes a master of himself."

## Neoplatonic Yoga

Plotinus' popularity earned him the jealousy of many a would-be rival. Olympius of Alexandria, a sort of Egyptian "black tantric" (sorcerer), launched a psychic attack against the philosopher. Plotinus admitted he actually felt the negative energies hurled at him; he reported his aura momentarily "squeezed like a money-bag being pulled tight." Olympius had placed a curse that caused a set of horrible symptoms to manifest in Plotinus' body. When those very symptoms started showing up in his own body instead, the sorcerer quickly stopped his attacks.

In one of the best-known episodes in Plotinus' life, an Egyptian priest invited the philosopher to the temple of Isis in Rome, promising to show him a vision of his guardian spirit. Many people in this era believed in the literal existence of guardian angels, but Plotinus saw the matter differently. He taught that each of us contains many worlds within ourselves, some of which we're conscious of and some of which we're not. The beings some claim to "channel" are not actually separate entities, according to Plotinus, but represent aspects of our own higher awareness, offering us guidance and protection. When the priest summoned Plotinus' guardian, expecting a spirit to appear, a brilliant light appeared instead. Plotinus' students took this as further evidence that their master was so advanced in meditation, he lived almost continually in pure divine light.

The Oracle at Delphi is famous for its simple advice: "Know thyself." Plotinus took this suggestion seriously. He advised his disciples, "Close your eyes and awaken to another way of seeing. This is a skill everyone possesses but few choose to use."

Would-be spiritual teachers who talked the talk but didn't walk the walk did not impress Plotinus. Longinus was chief minister to Zenobia of Palmyra (the famous warrior queen who gave the Romans so much trouble); he was also a fellow student of Plotinus' teacher, Ammonius Saccas. Longinus was widely recognized as one of the most knowledgeable men of his day. Though his essays were excellent, Longinus was not doing his inner work—he wrote about mystical realities but didn't make an effort to experience them directly. "Longinus is a scholar, not a philosopher," Plotinus commented dryly. For Plotinus, philosophy (literally "the love of wisdom") was not just an intellectual exercise; it was a living mystical quest.

In the phrase most associated with Plotinus today, the master spoke of spiritual life as "the flight of the alone to the Alone." We are alone because we focus our attention almost exclusively outward on people and things that seem to be "other" than ourselves. They may even seem threatening. So we become lonely, selfish, and fearful. The Supreme Reality is "Alone" because there is nothing other than itself—all beings, all worlds, all times, all possibilities are contained within it. When the lonely lower self soars upward into the sky of the infinitely expansive Higher Self, we experience a spiritual exhilaration that is all-embracing. Plotinus died in 270 C.E. of a painful, lingering disease. His last words, whispered to the physician who was with him, were, "Try to unite the divinity in yourself with the divine in all things." With his last breath Plotinus spoke of yoga, "union with the divine."

Was Plotinus a yogi? If a *jnana* yogi is an adept who uses his discriminating intelligence to strip himself of everything that isn't divine and who masters the states of samadhi in order to establish himself in unitary awareness, the answer is unequivocally yes. Yet many modern Western scholars doubt that Plotinus was influenced by the yoga tradition, in spite of the fact that we know from such early Christian writers as Hippolytus that yoga philosophy was being taught in Rome during Plotinus' lifetime. Besides, Plotinus knew at least enough about yoga to risk his life trying to reach India to learn even more. Academic symposia have been convened in an attempt to explain away the remarkable parallels between Plotinus and Indian thought.

In his *Enneads*, Plotinus cataloged the different states of samadhi, and how to attain them, as clearly as if he were writing a commentary on the *Yoga Sutra*. However, he never mentions India and refers only to the works of great Western spiritual masters such as Aristotle, Parmenides, and particularly Plato. For these reasons most scholars believe that although Plotinus may have been aware of Indian doctrines, he saw his work within the context of the Greek tradition expounded by Plato. This was his *sampradaya*, as the yogis would call it, his "spiritual lineage."

Even if Plotinus had never heard of India, his one-pointed contemplations would have led him into the states of samadhi because they are real realms any inner explorer will encounter, just as anyone investigating the outer world will ultimately discover the same laws of physics. According to the yoga adepts, Lord Shiva, the Inner Self of the universe, is the supreme guru of all yogis, whether they are Siberian shamans, Hopi Indians, or Egyptian contemplatives teaching philosophy in Rome.

There is an amazing story about Augustine of Hippo, one of the primary framers of the Christian faith. On his deathbed, as he gazed into the unblinking eyes of eternity, he didn't ask his students to bring him the Gospels or any Christian homilies. Instead he asked for his beloved copy of Plotinus' *Enneads*. In the face of death, Augustine's sectarian bias fell away, and he turned to the eternal truths of the great mystical tradition underlying *all* faiths. Of this undying tradition Plotinus was perhaps the most articulate and inspired master in Western spiritual history.

# CHAPTER FIFTEEN

# The Work of Enlightenment

### IAMBLICHUS

WHAT DOES IT TAKE TO ACTUALLY become enlightened? To step off the wheel of reincarnation and walk in the light? The yogis, swamis, buddhas, and bodhisattvas of India were by no means the only ancients who pondered these questions and set off on an active quest for down-to-earth answers. From Luxor in Egypt to Babylon in Persia, from the Druids in Britain to the Taoists in China, men and women sought the keys to the kingdom of illumined awareness. Let's turn back the clock eighteen hundred years to catch a glimpse of another determined soul who paved a path to light.

Picture the east coast of the Mediterranean; between the sea and the rivers of Mesopotamia lay the enormous cosmopolitan Roman province of Syria. It was the third century C.E.; Islam had not yet been born, and Christianity still hadn't made much of an impact there. Yamliku (whose Semitic name means "God is king") was growing up in the Syrian city of Chalcis. He was the wealthy son of a prominent family—one of his Arab ancestors had actually founded the city. Historians remember him as Iamblichus (the Latin version of his name), one of the most respected spiritual masters of the ancient Western world.

As a young man, Iamblichus was fascinated by the spirituality teeming all around him. There were Zoroastrian Magi with their mystic rites to the sacred fire, the Chaldeans with their astonishing tiers of angels and demons, and visitors from Egypt chanting mantras from the beginning of time. There were psychics and astrologers, philosophers and initiates, ascetics and ecstatics, huge public temples and secretive mystery schools. There were also, of course, brahmins and gymnosophists from India. Indians had been a fixture in the West since at least the time of Caesar Augustus.

Iamblichus' spiritual interests led him to one of the most respected teachers of his time, the learned and influential philosopher Porphyry. Like Iamblichus, Porphyry was from a part of the world the Greeks considered Oriental: he had been born in Tyre, a city in Lebanon. Porphyry was the best-known disciple of the late Neoplatonic master Plotinus.

Plotinus had been a saint and a meditation adept of the highest caliber. Porphyry, however, was an intellectual who spent most of his time writing and teaching. The difference between Plotinus and Porphyry was something like that between Jesus and Paul of Tarsus, who wrote many of the books in the New Testament. Jesus was the true master, but it was Paul who spread Jesus' gospel far beyond the confines of his primarily Jewish following. Paul himself was a fallible human being who was often severely criticized by the Christians of his own time. Porphyry was Plotinus' premier apostle, and we owe him an enormous debt of gratitude for preserving the master's words for future generations. Yet Porphyry himself, like Paul, struggled with the practical dimensions of spiritual life.

Porphyry was committed to a spiritual method that yoga students call *jnana* yoga or "the path of the intellect." By painstakingly directing his attention inward toward the transcendent source of all phenomena, Porphyry hoped to permanently root his awareness in the One, the perfect unity behind all existence. To help himself in this difficult process, he honed his ability to think analytically and carefully studied the traditions of spiritual masters such as Plato and Pythagoras.

Iamblichus, however, was deeply dissatisfied with Porphyry's overly analytical approach. He couldn't help noting that occasionally Porphyry, his immense intellect notwithstanding, would slip into states of near-suicidal depression. This observation left the young student from Chalcis with serious questions. What good is a spiritual path if it doesn't transform the personality? How can a master be enlightened if he's still a slave to his emotions? Is there a spiritual methodology that not only carries one's awareness to the One but also illumines his entire nature?

At this time in history, the Greeks were famous throughout the Western world for their brilliant philosophy. But Iamblichus decided that philosophy alone is not enough to lead anyone to enlightenment. He complained that since the spectacular success of some of the more rationally oriented Greek schools, there was too much emphasis on *theology*, which in Greek means "talk about God," and not enough on *theurgy*, which means "working toward God"—actively doing the spiritual practices that actually produce real inner transformation.

But what were these practices? Searching for answers, Iamblichus turned back to the ancient traditions that had so deeply impressed him as a child: the Egyptian, Chaldean, and Assyrian systems. (The Chaldeans and Assyrians flourished in the part of the world we call Iran and Iraq today.) The great masters of these traditions didn't just talk the talk. They walked the walk, radiating spiritual power and emanating tangible blessing force. What were these extraordinary men and women doing that Porphyry seemed to have missed?

## Three Steps to Spirit

Iamblichus noted that the ancient traditions incorporated three tiers of spiritual practice. First there were rituals. During these sacred rites the seeker aligned himself with the cosmic forces that drove the universe. It wasn't possible to control these powerful forces, but it *was* possible to become a conduit for their wisdom and blessing energy. During ritual practices the seeker invited a higher power to illumine his awareness and guide his actions.

Iamblichus was not naive about this type of spiritual work. He recognized that too many people who try to channel a higher power are in fact only deluding themselves, or even worse, mistakenly inviting ignorant or malevolent forces into their lives. He wrote at length about this in his classic work *On the Mysteries*, explaining how seekers can tell if their spiritual experiences are authentic. Real experiences exalt the soul, not the ego, and lead to the greater good of all humanity. Rituals must be performed with humility and virtue, or they can all too readily turn into sorcery, he warned.

The second tier of spiritual practices involved working with mantras. Iamblichus' understanding of mantras was astonishingly similar to that of the Indian yogis. Mantras, he explained, were not words invented by human beings but divine sounds that emanate from higher levels of reality. The reason mantras aren't formulated in a language we can understand is that they're designed to transport us out of our conceptual minds and into higher states of consciousness. They bypass the intellect as they carry us back toward their source. Unfortunately for us today, the ancients never wrote down their mantras—they were far too sacred—so we don't know which ones Iamblichus himself used.

Iamblichus also encouraged his students to engage in devotional singing, chanting mantras and divine names. "Devotional music," he wrote, "elevates our spirit because it reminds us of the divine harmonies experienced in higher worlds before we entered our physical body."

The third level of spiritual practice can't be described in words, Iamblichus admitted, and is beyond the capability of most people anyway. It involved releasing all physical and mental activity and resting in pure awareness itself. This condition, called *henosis*, or "abiding in the One," was the state yogis call samadhi. Interestingly, Iamblichus didn't believe we could attain the highest state through our own efforts alone. Ultimate states, he felt, are beyond the reach of the human mind. We can experience them only if the divine itself reaches downward and, out of pure grace, lifts us to itself. The best we can do is prepare ourselves for this experience through daily spiritual practice in which we sincerely invoke the divine presence with rituals, mantras, and meditation.

Iamblichus also wrote that there are three types of humans who reincarnate on Earth for different purposes. The lowest class of souls are ignorant and selfish and are punished by karmic law. The middle level have begun to awaken to spiritual life and are sincerely working to purify and improve themselves. The highest grade of souls, however, are not here to learn but to serve. They are already enlightened but return to the physical plane to protect, heal, and guide the rest of us.

## Tantra in the West

What makes the precious few of Iamblichus' works that have survived to the present so exceptionally fascinating is that they provide conclusive evidence that the basic principles of Tantra were understood in the West eighteen hundred years ago, just as they were in India.

In Sanskrit, the word *tantra* refers to the "warp and weft" of the universe, the threads with which reality is woven. These threads are interlinked in ways that have a surprising underlying logic. Tantrics manipulate these links to produce effects that can seem magical to the uninitiated. Iamblichus specifically described the energetic processes that shape reality as a sort of "rhythmic weaving." His rituals incorporated gems with certain qualities, plants, fragrances, and other carefully chosen objects designed to synchronize the participants with particular cosmic forces, much as Indian tantrics do to this day. Every object, he believed, bore the "signature" (*synthema* in Greek) of the cosmic entity that projected it into manifestation. The resonances between specific objects or mantras and their source in consciousness were called *sympatheia*. They could be used to correct imbalances in the practitioner's psyche as well as to help resolve practical problems in life.

For example, black seeds, lapis lazuli, or dark pieces of rough cloth might be used to align oneself ritually with the dark and destructive energies associated with the planet Saturn. By ritually harmonizing with Saturn's qualities, one could make peace with these energies, overcoming saturnine imbalances such as the depression from which Porphyry suffered. However, Iamblichus counseled, performing rituals without understanding their subtle operational principles was as useless as studying philosophy without doing spiritual practice.

For Iamblichus, as for yogis and tantrics in India to this day, the entryway to effective spiritual practice was tradition, the living lineage of masters who pass on their experience from generation to generation. Iamblichus noted that some Greeks would simply make up mantras, but these didn't seem to have much effect. "Mantras used from time immemorial by the Egyptians and Assyrians were given to them directly by higher beings. These cultures have preserved their connection with the higher intelligences over the centuries," Iamblichus believed. Rites and mantras received from a higher source by sages in deep states of spiritual communion were highly energized and retained their power through constant sincere practice by generations of devotees. These rites were the keys to the inner worlds and allowed human practitioners to align themselves as co-creators with the gods. After all, Iamblichus wrote, "Humans are the lowest form of divine being."

For the gods, to "think" a thing was for it to become a reality. For us, merely to bring the concept of a beautiful house, a horse, or a lover to mind instantly creates an image on our mental screen. The physical universe itself is, in a sense, the mental screen of the gods. They call plants or planets, atoms or solar systems into existence merely by "thinking" or "naming" them. (You may remember that even in the Bible God merely speaks the words "Let there be light," and light appears [Genesis 1:3].) Most of us retain this ability only in our fantasies. But through properly performed rituals and correctly pronounced mantras, we can activate the *sympatheia*, or "sympathetic links," between ourselves and higher realities. When we finally master this process we too may be able to "speak" a thought and see it become a physical reality.

## Life beyond Space and Time

While absorbed in the performance of rituals, or while meditating on mantras, some people actually have visions of divine beings. But these spiritual entities don't really have bodies, Iamblichus reminded his students. Rather, they exist as formless consciousness and will. Most of us can't even begin to imagine the state of awareness of these great souls. So our minds present them to us cloaked in a form we can more easily grasp, such as a vision of a favorite saint, an angel, or a deity.

The gods exist outside time and space, Iamblichus taught. They experience the past, present, and future simultaneously, so nothing is unknown to them. For us, "the lowest form of divine being," though, the future is concealed. This forces us—since we are unsure of the outcome of our actions—to carefully distinguish between good and evil and make ethical choices. When we are finally granted the state of enlightenment, we will be able to experience the unitary nature of space and time just as divine beings do.

Porphyry and Iamblichus fought a very public battle over their contrasting approaches to spirituality, critiquing each other in their books. Porphyry argued that enlightenment is a purely internal process and that rituals are useless. For students of Indian history, it's amazing how closely their intellectual duel parallels that between the Vedantins, who championed the path of the intellect, and the Mimamsas, who insisted that the continued performance of ancient rites was absolutely necessary. To this day Indian tantrics in the Samaya schools also condemn ritual practice, while Kaula tantrics claim it's the very essence of spiritual life.

Spiritual masters, such as Plotinus in the third century and the South Indian sage Ramana Maharshi in the twentieth, demonstrate that enlightenment is entirely possible without any ritual practice at all. Yet for those for whom the direct path of purely internal practice is too difficult, or simply too unappealing, the tantric path outlined by Iamblichus ultimately leads to the same goal.

It's mildly amusing to read scholarly essays by modern professors guessing at the nature of the practices in which Iamblichus was involved. If they spent a few weeks in India, they would have ample opportunity to watch many similar tantric techniques still being used today.

## The Divine Iamblichus

Iamblichus' school was probably located in the Syrian city of Apamea, but his influence was felt from Athens to Alexandria to Rome itself. The Roman emperor Julian once exclaimed, "I'd rather have a few words from Iamblichus than all the gold in Lydia!"

Iamblichus was one of the only three spiritual masters in the Western world whom the ancients honored with the title *theios,* "divine." (The other two were Pythagoras and Plato.) A *theios* was believed to have been inspired directly by God for the benefit of all humanity. Some of the greatest minds of the next few centuries were profoundly inspired by Iamblichus, so much so that they eagerly took up meditation and spiritual practice. You'll learn about one of these, the amazing Turkish master Proclus, in a later chapter.

After Iamblichus, just talking about higher dimensions of reality was no longer enough. He helped men and women of the West understand that by actively working for it, divine reality could be more than a topic of philosophical debate; it could be a living experience.

# CHAPTER SIXTEEN

# The Shepherd of Men

## HERMES TRISMEGISTUS

IN 1460 COSIMO DE MEDICI stumbled across a manuscript that rocked the foundations of Europe. The wealthy Italian nobleman had been eagerly collecting writings of great Hellenistic masters such as Plotinus and "the divine Plato." It was a big job: memory of the pre-Christian masters had been largely expunged in Western Europe by religious zealots anxious to erase all traces of wisdom that weren't sanctioned by the Church. The resulting pogrom against honest spiritual inquiry, science, and medicine had plunged Europe into the Dark Ages.

A tiny fraction of the ancient writings survived the burning of libraries and persecution of non-Christian teachers. Some of these texts had been translated into Arabic and preserved in Islamic countries, which were far more tolerant in those days than Judeo-Christian cultures. Others had been saved in small personal collections. Cosimo searched the world for these treasures and had them translated into Latin, the language of educated people in his day. It was this rediscovery of ancient Greek masters that helped galvanize the leading minds of Europe, ignite the Renaissance, and propel Europe out of its Dark Ages and into the modern period.

But it was in 1460 that a monk, knowing Cosimo paid handsomely for old books, arrived from northern Greece with a manuscript that would send Cosimo reeling. It was the *Corpus Hermetica*, a collection of discourses by the legendary Egyptian master Hermes. One ancient Greek master after another, from Thales to Pythagoras to Plato, had acknowledged his indebtedness to the priest philosophers of Egypt. And now here was the long-lost book of Hermes himself, the greatest spiritual teacher Egypt ever produced. Cosimo instantly summoned his translator, Marsilio Ficino, and ordered him to lay aside his vitally important work on Plato's dialogues. He was to begin at once translating the writings of Hermes Trismegistus, "Thrice Great Hermes."

Ficino could scarcely believe his luck. Here were the wisdom teachings of a master from time immemorial that outlined the secret doctrines of the oldest and most spiritual culture in the Western Hemisphere. The ancient master was called Tehowti by the Egyptians (mispronounced "Thoth" by the Greeks), but had long been styled Hermes by Greek and Latin writers of old who mentioned his name with deepest reverence. He had been Egypt's greatest priest, scientist, and engineer and was thus "three times great." He was also the consummate magician, a man who understood and commanded the hidden forces of nature.

Who would have imagined a lengthy work by this spiritual giant still existed? Cosimo waited with bated breath as each text in the collection was translated from the Greek. He was not well and couldn't bear to die without reading this remarkable document. Ficino worked day and night, completing the work before Cosimo passed away. His translation of the *Corpus Hermetica* would become one of the most influential books of the next hundred years, running through sixteen editions and serving as a sort of alternate Bible for Renaissance freethinkers.

Today you'll search in vain for scholars who seriously believe the *Corpus Hermetica* was written in vast antiquity by a superman named Thoth. Internal textual evidence suggests it was originally composed in Greek, not translated into Greek from Egyptian, as Cosimo believed. Clearly, different sections were written by different authors, some writing perhaps as early as the fourth century B.C.E., others maybe as late as the third century C.E. (There is a slim chance some of the essays may be older. Greek-speaking colonists built their own city in Egypt in the seventh century B.C.E. and may already have familiarized themselves with Thoth's tradition then.) Modern scholars debate how much of the Hermetic writings actually are inspired by Egyptian doctrine, and how much represents what Greek speakers simply imagined the ancient Egyptian teachings must have been. In antiquity, however, there was no such confusion. The ancient Greeks were convinced the *Corpus Hermetica* were authentic transmissions of millennia-old Egyptian wisdom. Scholars today may claim these texts were inspired by Plato, but Plato himself suggested he got his doctrines from the Egyptians.

Ancient Greeks were well acquainted with Egyptian culture. Herodotus, the famous Greek historian, admitted that much of Greek religion had been borrowed directly from Egypt. This exchange began in earnest when Alexander the Great invaded Egypt in 332 B.C.E. Surprisingly, he was welcomed into Egypt because he drove out the hated Persians, who had ruled there for two hundred years. One of Alexander's generals, Ptolemy Soter, set himself up as pharaoh in 323 B.C.E. Egypt remained under Greek control until 30 B.C.E., when the Romans launched their own successful invasion. Cleopatra, the last of the Ptolemaic line, committed suicide after her plan to escape to India was thwarted; the country was quickly absorbed into the Roman Empire under

Caesar Augustus. However, many educated Egyptians were by now steeped in Greek culture and continued to write and speak in the Greek language for centuries.

It appears that the *Corpus Hermetica* and other related Hermetic literature, such as a startling document titled "The Virgin of the World," were written by native Egyptians borrowing the language and philosophical vocabulary of their Greek rulers. These texts, brimming with mystical insights, greatly expand the spiritual contents of hieroglyphic texts painted on tomb walls. They also dovetail in important respects with early Christianity. In fact, Hermetic treatises were included in the ancient Christian library unearthed near Nag Hammadi, Egypt, in 1945.

Reading the Hermetic treatises today, it's easy to see why Cosimo was thrilled. After two thousand years they remain perhaps the most exciting and inspiring spiritual texts ever composed in the Western world, rivaled only by Plotinus' *Enneads*—and Plotinus, you'll remember, was from Egypt. Let's take a look at this extraordinary mystical literature, the last legacy of Egypt's ancient spiritual wisdom.

## The Divine Shepherd

"I am the shepherd of men, the Supreme Awareness. I am always with you, and I already know what you desire," begins the *Poimandres*, the amazing opening discourse in the *Corpus Hermetica* (or C.H. I).

"I want to know God and I want to understand the universe," the disciple responds.

"Focus your mind—I will teach you," promises Poimandres, the divine teacher after whom this essay is named. "Here is what you must understand: that within you which sees and hears is divine awareness itself. The highest consciousness inside you is nothing other than the Supreme Reality. There is no difference between your innermost being and God. Realize what you really are."

"But if we're divine beings, why do we find ourselves in physical bodies, completely unaware of our real nature?" the disciple demands.

Poimandres explains that before the beginning of time the Supreme Being manifested out of himself a creator god. That which is beyond space, time, and thought, that which is completely unlimited, emitted a more limited version of itself, a vast intelligence capable of working within the framework of causality. This Creator guided the formation of the universe in the infinite field of its awareness.

Then the Supreme Being emitted one more entity, a beloved child, the first human. This original human being was an androgynous, bodiless mind. Perceiving that the Creator had formed a dazzling physical universe, this new human wanted to create something beautiful too.

In the shimmering waters of material manifestation the human saw a reflection of itself. "How wonderful," it thought. "What would it be like to inhabit that form?" Whatever the entity thought instantly became reality, so the idea had no sooner occurred to it than nature reached out and embraced it, and the human found itself encased in matter. It now had a higher mind capable of reason and intuition, a lower mind capable of sensing the world around it, a physical body capable of interacting with matter, and life energy to animate it. More than that, this androgynous being had two physical bodies, not one. It was now a male and a female, who kept trying to unite back into each other. They didn't succeed, but their efforts did have a side effect: they wound up populating the world with numerous other males and females.

"Those who remember their real nature, recognizing the

divine awareness within, attain the greatest good. Knowing they come from a world of light, they return to that immortal radiance. But those who prefer the life of the body find themselves lost and confused, and grieve when they lose their body at death," Poimandres teaches.

"You're saying the self-aware person recognizes his real nature. But *how?*" the disciple asks.

"I, the Supreme Awareness, am always present to those who are good and kind, pure and full of reverence. I guide them back to their innate nature, helping them quickly recognize their true Self. But those who are violent and disrespectful, unthinking and greedy, do not feel me near. These people go on desiring more and more from the world, craving lasting happiness it can never give them. Their unfulfillable desires cause them endless torment.

"The path back to your Divine Father leads beyond your body, from which you must shift your attention. Your thoughts, feelings, and sensations arise from contact with matter; you must release them. Move upward through the seven spheres of your being into the highest region of your awareness. Let go of everything else and merge your awareness in God alone. Do this not for your own sake, but so that you can help others find their way also."

Under Poimandres' direction, the disciple ascends to the heights of consciousness and actually achieves God-realization. Spiritually empowered, he returns to the material plane to guide others. "Why have you surrendered to death, you men and women who are capable of immortality?" he challenges the crowds. "Wake up! Stop this ignorant behavior, step out of the shadows, and claim your birthright: eternal life." Most people ignore the disciple, but a few listen eagerly and begin to tread the spiritual path. In the evening Poimandres' disciple gives thanks to God, the father of all, and, closing his eyes in meditation, enjoys the vision of truth.

Today few of us Westerners are familiar with ancient Egyptian religion. Many of us, though, have taken yoga classes or read New Age–oriented books on Eastern philosophy. Reading a text like the *Poimandres* is a startling experience for us because its account is so nearly identical to the wisdom tradition of India. Even the name *Poimandres,* "the divine shepherd," or "the shepherd of men," reminds us of Indian names for God, such as Govinda or Gopala ("cowherd"—in India cows, not sheep, were the most prized animals) and Pashupati ("lord of the cattle"). We souls are the flock the Lord cares for.

The *Poimandres* describes the Absolute projecting a creator god out of itself. In India Brahma the Creator is said to arise from a lotus growing out of the navel of Vishnu, the Supreme Being. In Egyptian art going back as far as the eighteenth dynasty, the creator god is sometimes drawn emerging from a lotus.

Needless to say, the identity of our Inner Self with the Supreme Self is a central tenet of much of Indian mystical thought. The "seven spheres" through which we must lift our consciousness before merging in the Supreme remind us of India's seven chakras, which, like the Hermetic spheres, are keyed to the seven classical planets.

Even the five bodies that encase our innermost being are identical in the two traditions. The tenth text in the *Corpus Hermetica* (or C.H. X), often called *The Key*, describes these five "envelopes" of consciousness: "The innermost Spirit is carried about in this way: the *nous* is in the *logos,* the *logos* in the *psyche,* the *psyche* in the *pneuma,* and the *pneuma* in the *soma.*" What do these Greek words and their exact Sanskrit equivalents mean?

| Greek | Sanskrit | Definition |
|-------|----------|------------|
| *soma* | *annamaya kosha* | physical body |
| *pneuma* | *pranamaya kosha* | vital force or energy body |
| *psyche* | *manomaya kosha* | sensory awareness, everyday mind |
| *logos* | *vijnanamaya kosha* | intellect, higher reasoning faculty |
| *nous* | *anandamaya kosha* | intuitive awareness, mystical consciousness |

Incredibly, *The Key* echoes in precise detail the doctrine of India's ancient *Taittiriya Upanishad,* which describes five progressively subtler *koshas,* or "sheaths," enveloping consciousness. *The Key* goes on to call reason the "shroud" of mystical awareness, while our ordinary sensory awareness wears the vital force "like armor." The vital force is then the "governor" of the physical body, a statement with which homeopaths, acupuncturists, martial artists, and yogis would still agree today.

Are these Greek terms really prefigured in Egyptian religion? In very old Egyptian texts, the physical body is called *khat,* the vital force is called *ka,* the mind is *ba,* the reasoning faculty is *djed,* and the intuitive self or being of light is *akh.* Fascinatingly, even so technical a Sanskrit term as *karmashaya,* the portion of the intuitive body in which one's karma is stored, has an Egyptian equivalent, *ab,* represented as a vase in tomb art. It is weighed after death to determine the individual's postmortem destiny. The Hellenized Egyptians (or perhaps Egyptianized Greeks) who wrote the *Corpus Hermetica* were probably recalling this extremely ancient tradition common to both Egypt and India.

## Echoes of India

The Hermetic tradition has much in common with yoga. The Hermetists refused to eat meat. According to a text called the *Asclepius*, they followed their lectures with "a pure vegetarian meal." According to Porphyry, Hermes taught that the flesh of animals killed violently shouldn't be eaten because the aftershocks of the animal's terror remained in the meat and would hamper an aspirant's spiritual growth.

As in yoga, the reality of reincarnation is continually affirmed in the Hermetic teachings. In *The Mixing Bowl* (C.H. IV), Hermes challenges his disciple, "Do you understand how many bodies, how many personalities, and how many planetary cycles we must pass through in order to reach the One?"

This world is a remarkable creation of higher consciousness, but it isn't stable and therefore, in a sense, isn't ultimately real. "All we see here are shadows and illusions," Hermes stated in *Perfection Exists in God Alone* (C.H. VI), mirroring the Indian doctrine of *maya*. In some passages the Hermetic texts praise the material universe, but in others they remind the aspirant that overattachment to this world inevitably leads to suffering.

If the Hermetists were conscious of the illusoriness of the world, they were also well aware of the reality of karma. In an excerpt preserved for us by Stobaeus (an anthologist from the early fifth century who collected sayings from antiquity for his son), Hermes explained, "Necessity rules the universe, but justice rules humanity. The stars and elemental forces must obey the laws of nature. But men and women have free will, and therefore are able to make mistakes. Karma, the rule of justice, corrects those who err. Humanity is subject to fate due to the forces at work at the time of their birth, and to destiny due to their actions in this life." In India fate is called *prarabdha karma*, the karma we've amassed as a result of our actions in previous lives. Destiny is called *kriya-mana* karma, the consequences of our behavior in this life.

In another excerpt Hermes explained even more clearly, "Those beings who act on the basis of higher consciousness act in accordance with providence, that is, with God's will. Creatures and things with little or no self-awareness act according to necessity, that is, the dictates of nature. But beings with free will are subject to fate," that is, the law of karma.

The Egyptians were famous for their mantras, though these were different from Indian mantras. They appear to have been primarily vowel sounds vocalized to create specific effects in consciousness. Just as Hindus call Sanskrit *devanagari*, "the language of the gods," so too Egyptian priests held that their ancient language was sacred, a gift from the god Thoth. In *Definitions to King Ammon* (C.H. XVI), Asclepius says, "The very sound of the words we use contains the energy of the objects we're describing. The Greeks use empty words, but we Egyptians use words that are full of energy." The Hindus developed a sophisticated science of language, which they traced back to the goddess Vak (literally "Word"). Apparently the Egyptians had a similar tradition, originating from Thoth.

Did the Graeco-Egyptian tradition recognize higher states of consciousness similar to those that the Indian yogis describe? Apparently so. *The Key* (C.H. X) tells us, "Most of us aren't pure enough to see unchanging, inexpressible divine perfection, the one true beauty, with our inner eye. Only in the moment when you no longer speak or even think can it be known. The senses and mind must be absolutely still. When you're immersed in that experience, you can't see or hear anything else or even move your body. You sit completely still, your body and mind both unmoving. When that living stillness permeates you, your consciousness is drawn upward, and you're absorbed into divine awareness." This is as fine a description of *nirvikalpa samadhi*, the yogic state of one-pointed absorption in pure awareness, as you'll find in any yoga text.

Exactly as in India, the Hermetists emphasized the vital importance of finding a Self-realized teacher who can transmit the force of his or her realization directly to the prepared disciple. Hermetic texts such as *The Eight Reveal the Nine*, found at Nag Hammadi, demonstrate in some detail how this is done. *Ignorance*, another tract from the *Corpus Hermetica* (C.H. VII), explains, "Ignorance is flooding the whole world, preventing the souls here from taking refuge in the state of spiritual liberation. If you don't want to sink in this ocean of ignorance, find a guru who can lead you to that true knowledge which can't be seen with the eyes but must be experienced directly with the heart and mind. You will need to shift your awareness beyond your body—your garment of ignorance, your portable tomb—which prevents you from experiencing a higher reality." It's the spiritual teacher's job to help a disciple achieve this.

"Since becoming still," the disciple mentioned in *Born Again* (C.H. XIII) reports, "I am in heaven and on Earth, in the water and the air. I am in plants and animals, in every being embodied and disembodied. I am everywhere." Higher states of awareness have opened the inner doors to cosmic consciousness.

Hermes described his own experience in the same text. "Through the grace of God I experience the Supreme Reality. I exist far beyond my body in a state of pure awareness. I have been reborn in the immortal form of consciousness itself. Though you're looking at me you don't see what I am. You can't understand what I have become." The guru has virtually become God, merging into universal awareness.

The ultimate guru, according to the yogic tradition, is in fact the Supreme Consciousness itself. Hermes agreed. In *The Universal Mind* (C.H. XII) Hermes wrote, "Divine Consciousness reveals its grandeur to the soul it leads. Like a good physician who takes a scalpel and cauterizer to a sick patient, the Inner Spirit inflicts pain on a soul in order to pull it away from its preoccupation with passing pleasures, and guide it to a higher reality." In the *Corpus Hermetica* the name *Hermes* refers both to a human guru and to the Supreme Consciousness because in the state of God-realization, the two become one. This state of unity is described in many Sanskrit texts, such as the *Guru Gita*.

A human being experiencing this level of awareness may seem crazy to normal people. "Those who exist in the state of God-realization may appear mad and are ridiculed by the ignorant. They may be hated and despised, even murdered, by those who simply can't understand higher states," according to *On Understanding* (C.H. IX). In India the tradition of *avadhuts*, or crazy-seeming sages, is very ancient, but there these extraordinary men and women are honored, not persecuted.

Amazingly, even sexual practices well known from the Indian tantric tradition are mentioned in the *Asclepius*, a Hermetic text preserved in Latin.

## Wisdom of Hermes

What did Hermetic spiritual practice consist of?

"Only one path leads from here to the Supreme Beauty: knowledge combined with deepest reverence."

"When you understand that this beautiful cosmos is the product of God, who is himself the Supreme Beauty, you will work to sustain and enhance the beauty you see here with your full attention and respect."

"To honor God means this: constant, attentive service."

"To love God with a pure heart and mind, to honor this world God has created, and to surrender to God's will with gratitude, this is authentic spiritual practice."

"This, my son, is the only path that leads to Reality. Our enlightened ancestors followed this path and attained perfection. It is a sacred road, but it's difficult to follow while you're still in your body. Your soul will constantly be at war with itself, the part of you that longs to ascend to higher dimensions struggling continually with the part that wants to remain here. If the lower part wins, the pure soul is held prisoner by the lesser self and tormented by feelings of attraction and repulsion. If the higher part wins, you will live a blessed life and die a blessed death, for when it departs from this world your soul will know its way home."

We know the Hermetists made use of rituals, visualization, meditation, astrology, and prayer. But in any esoteric tradition, specific details about spiritual practice are hardly ever written down; instead they're transmitted orally from teacher to student. Yet hints about the Hermetic path have survived to tantalize us. We know that the Graeco-Egyptian sages carefully mapped out the way the different dimensions of the cosmos flow out from the Absolute Reality, so that they can follow this trail back to the Supreme, exactly as the Sankhya yogis did in India. The forces of ignorance that hold back the soul are overcome by knowing the steps and stages of return to the primordial reality outside space and time. However, intellectual knowledge by itself isn't enough. A radical transformation of the entire personality must occur. The *Corpus Hermetica* insists the individual must be "born again" while still in the body, an image Christians would borrow.

In *The Mixing Bowl* (C.H. IV), Hermes explained that God gave all humans the power to reason, but we were not all born with access to higher consciousness. "This is a prize he wants us to work for ourselves." Hermes used a metaphor that Plato (who, you'll remember, studied in Egypt) also used: higher consciousness is contained in a vast bowl. "If you have the power to do so, if you understand the real reason you were born, then immerse your awareness in this bowl. If you can do this, you will know everything in heaven and on Earth, and even more. Once you have tasted that state of awareness, this world will lose its power over you, and you will direct your entire being toward the One." Today many of us think of baptism as having water sprinkled on our heads, or perhaps immersing ourselves in the river Jordan. In the Hermetic tradition baptism meant immersing our individual awareness in the "vast bowl" of universal consciousness. This is what Hermes meant by being "born again."

Today Western religion places tremendous emphasis on faith, which some say is enough to save us. Hermes taught that self-purification and mastery of the mind are also necessary. Understanding the nature of consciousness is critical because the Supreme Being himself *is* pure consciousness. "God contains everything in himself, not in a spatial sense, but just as mind holds everything within it. Look at it this way: imagine yourself in India, and instantly your mind is there. Consciousness is not restrained by having to pass through space. Indeed, if you imagine yourself at the farthest edge of the universe, your mind is already there. If you have this power, how much more so must God! He contains the cosmos like an image in his mind. In order to understand God you will have to become like him. Expand your awareness till it encompasses the entire universe. Contain everything within yourself at once. Only then can you begin to comprehend the Supreme Being." (This imagery may jog your memory because it's exactly the meditation technique Plotinus taught his students in Rome.)

Can the human mind really do this—actually experience divine awareness, not merely imagine it? Hermes' emphatic answer was yes. "Nothing is impossible for mind," he wrote in *The Universal Mind* (C.H. XII).

## The Good, the Bad, and the Beautiful

Why are we here? Why, for that matter, is the universe itself here? Very ancient Egyptian texts address these central questions, and the Hermetists passed these views on to later generations.

In extremely old accounts, such as the *Pyramid Texts*, Egyptian priests called the original human being Atum. It was neither male nor female, but somehow both, and had been shaped out of the primeval mud. Eventually the creator god split this creature into two, the original man and woman. Centuries later Hebrew sages would borrow this myth, still calling the original human Adam, or Adam Kadmon in Kabbalah. According to the book of Genesis, this Adam too was molded from clay, and the creator shaped two humans from it: the second Adam and his wife, Eve. But why did God bother to do this?

"God is completely beyond the ability of any being to cognize," states the *Corpus Hermetica*. "And yet he wants to be seen. So he emanated the universe in order that we might recognize him. He is constantly creating more wonders so his majesty can be appreciated."

In *The Sacred Discourse* (C.H. III), Hermes taught, "All the generations of humankind were created for these purposes: to know God, to understand the cosmic forces, to work skillfully with nature, to comprehend the difference between right and wrong, and to procreate so that more souls can join in this sacred work."

The *Asclepius* says, "God created a marvelous universe full of beauty and goodness. But there was no one other than himself to admire it! So he created the human soul, which inherited his self-awareness and mental power. However, this new being could not interact with the material world unless it had a physical body, so God shaped one for it. This dual being, with both a spiritual and a material nature, was placed here to wonder and worship, and to care for the natural world."

Addressing the charge that God sometimes seems to ignore our hopes and prayers, *The Key* (C.H. X) answers, "God doesn't ignore us. Far from it! He's very much aware of us and wants us to be attentively aware of him. Knowing God is the only way to salvation. It's the ascent up Mount Olympus." Many early Christians, called Gnostics, entirely agreed, though they called the mountain Calvary.

If the universe is holy, and our purpose here is sacred, why then is there so much evil in the world? "God does not create evil; we do. We perform evil actions out of our own free will," Hermes answered.

When a disciple argues that God should end evil, the Hermetic sage Asclepius answers, "God gave us the ability to avoid evil when he gave us awareness, wisdom, and understanding. When we use these innate powers, *we* free *ourselves* from evil."

"We have the power to choose," Hermes agreed in another excerpt. "It is completely within our power to choose the better or the worse. Unfortunately, the soul who chooses evil becomes even more bound to its perishable physical body, and even more constrained by the chains of karma."

Why did God create death? According to Hermes, "Death is not destruction. It just means that two things that were united, soul and body, are no longer connected. The soul, which can't be seen, passes back into the unseen." Asclepius explained that we are actually "enriched by mortality," because the mortal condition allows seen and unseen, spirit and matter, to interact freely. He went on to say that after death, a soul passes into a state commensurate with the level of purity it attained here on Earth. Malicious, violent souls suffer terribly after death. The sage warned that it's better to be punished for a crime in life than to face the consequences after death, because postmortem suffering is far worse. (Plutarch, you'll recall, said the same thing.) However, even good souls who nevertheless have not yet realized their divine nature must return to Earth, being born into a new physical body to master the lessons they were assigned. Only enlightened souls are free to leave this world system, if they so choose, and abide in superconscious dimensions.

There is another important component of spiritual life about which Hermes spoke: divine grace. It draws us upward "like a magnet draws iron." Hermes counseled his disciple to maintain physical and mental silence "so as not to obstruct the flow of grace" that descends from a realm beyond thought. When we make a sincere effort to stretch our souls toward Spirit, grace begins to act. On this inner journey, "Goodness will find you everywhere you go. You'll see it everywhere you look, even when and where you least expect it."

## The Divine Word

Christians know the Gospel of John opens with the verse "In the beginning was the Word, and the Word was with God, and the Word was God," but not all of them know what this passage actually means. In Egypt the doctrine of a divine word coequal with God through whom God creates and enlightens the world can be traced back to remote antiquity. The Greek-speaking Hermetists made much of this doctrine of the logos, the divine word.

The *Corpus Hermetica* defines this word as the creative energy of the Supreme Being, the power of divine thought. Through it God's "only begotten son" comes into existence. However, in the Hermetic tradition this special son specifically refers to the inner universe, the framework of the cosmos, which can be seen only with the mind. It is a repository of ideas and energies, some of which take concrete form and materialize as our physical universe. Hermes explained that this inner cosmos is made in God's image and is reflected, though imperfectly, in the externalized cosmos we see with our eyes. Humanity, in turn, is made in the image of the cosmos, reflecting inside itself the movement of the stars, the interplay of earth, wind, water, and fire, and the intelligence of the Cosmic Mind. All dimensions of being correspond to each other, so that the coming together of Jupiter and Mars in their heavenly orbits matches events on Earth of a similar symbolic type. It is because of these symbolic correspondences that the ancient sciences of magic and divination really do work.

But the stars signaled a sad hiatus for the wisdom of Egypt. The *Asclepius* prophesies a tragic fate for the ancient land. "You know, Asclepius, that Egypt is the very reflection of heaven, that everything appearing above has been re-created here below. Our country is the sacred temple of the world.

"Yet a time is coming when the divine wisdom entrusted to us will depart from here and return to heaven. Foreigners will enter our nation, condemn and destroy our ancient faith, and this most holy land will hold only corpses and tombs.

"O Egypt, only legends of your greatness will survive, and people of the future won't even believe them! Egyptians of the future will be like foreigners; they will speak our language but know nothing of our culture and spirituality. This country, which has always been regarded by the entire world as the model of wisdom and spirituality, will set instead a new standard of ignorance and irreverence.

"In the future people here will prefer shadows to light. They will no longer gaze upward at the stars with wonder and respect. Our teachings about the nature of soul will be ridiculed as pure superstition. Nothing holy will remain. There will only be violence, disrespect, and contempt for everything good.

"But one day our Divine Father, who wills only good for the world, will send a flood or fire or pestilence to destroy that world. Our wisdom will be restored and the people will cry out with gratitude. Nature itself will be made whole again as the souls here are reformed, and our land will once more reverberate with worship and wonder."

So said Hermes Trismegistus, three times great.

# CHAPTER SEVENTEEN

# The Golden Chain

## PROCLUS

PROCLUS WAS LUMINOUS. Those who actually knew him tell us that he appeared to shine, the clarity, benevolence, and high intelligence of his soul radiating visibly from his body. He had nearly died as a boy, but then he'd seen a brilliant light shining above him. It enveloped him, and he was cured instantly. Proclus spent the rest of his life in the quest for more and more light.

Proclus was born in Byzantium around 410 C.E. He could hardly have known at the time that he would be the last great link in the lineage the ancients called the Golden Chain, the stream of spiritual knowledge that entered Greece through Orpheus and Pythagoras, that flowed through Plato and Plotinus, and that poured so generously through Proclus' study manuals and lectures.

Proclus' father was an attorney. Proclus was groomed for the same profession and was sent to the best schools in Rome and Alexandria. But Athena, goddess of wisdom, appeared to him in a vision and advised him to go to her city to study philosophy instead. So at age nineteen he moved to Athens and became a student of Syrianus, then head of Plato's Academy, an institution that eight hundred years after Plato's death still dominated Greek letters. He was soon initiated into the spiritual practices of this lineage by Asclepigenia, one of the leading women teachers in the tradition. His innate spirituality and extraordinary intelligence so impressed Syrianus that when the master stepped down six years later, he named Proclus his successor. At twenty-five, Proclus became the youngest teacher ever to head the illustrious Academy.

Proclus' disciple Marinus tells us Proclus' capacity for work was nearly miraculous. He lectured as many as five times a day. Students poured in from around the empire, eager to attend his fascinating and inspiring classes. At the same time he served as administrator of the institution, wrote voluminously, and still made time for hours of spiritual practice every day. He slept very little, rising early to bathe and purify himself in the traditional manner, sit for prayer and meditation, and perform the rituals of his lineage. Like many, if not most, of the leading sages of Western antiquity, Proclus was a committed vegetarian. He was so respected in his community that he received an exorbitant salary (the equivalent of an incredible half million dollars a year), yet he lived as a semi-ascetic, using the money to support the school.

We're also told Proclus had a quick temper. He had little patience for stupidity and would flare up at students who failed to meet his high standards. Marinus says his anger would dissipate instantly once his point was made.

The master was himself an avid student not only of his own Platonic lineage but also of the Chaldean wisdom tradition (a major source of Kabbalah). The Chaldeans had brilliantly synthesized the traditions of the Indo-European natives of Persia (essentially Hinduism), the Zoroastrians (an offshoot of early Hinduism), and ancient Semitic traditions passed down from the Assyrians to the Babylonians to the Arabs and Jews. Generally scholars today argue that the most important Chaldean text known by the Greeks, the amazing *Chaldean Oracles*, was a forgery rather than an authentic Greek translation. Whether or not that's true (I personally think modern scholars go overboard in their attempt to discredit the Greeks' grasp of foreign traditions), Proclus appears to have based some of his ideas about the subtle planes of reality on Chaldean teachings. He wrote at length about other entities who exist in our universe, occasionally interacting with humans, whom today we call angels.

I don't think there's any New Ager today who hasn't heard the term *astral body*. Although knowledge of the subtle body had been around for centuries, Proclus coined this particular phrase (*astroeides oschema* in Greek). Our first body, he taught, is the one made of physical matter. It deteriorates at death. Our second body is our sensory mind, the usual jumble of thoughts we identify with, our "lower self." This survives death but isn't immortal. It's the third body, an astral or "starlike" body that Proclus says endures forever. This is our Higher Self, our rational and intuitive being. These three bodies make it possible for us to interact with the worlds of matter, of thought, and of highest cosmic dimensions, respectively.

Fascinatingly, Proclus also believed in the existence of avatars and bodhisattvas. He wrote of special pure souls who descend into physical bodies in order to serve humanity. They bring with them personal knowledge of higher realms and are able to redirect the minds of ordinary men and women toward states of increasing awareness. Because the highest reality is so far beyond what we normally experience, we need divine grace, whether from God himself or from special souls like these, to make the breakthrough to enlightenment.

## Western Wisdom

Proclus taught that in essence there is only one unitary reality, which is consciousness itself. This doesn't mean consciousness in the usual workaday sense, but an extremely rarified form of awareness beyond space and time, even beyond what we'd ordinarily think of as "being." The universe of our experience emanates outward from this Supreme Reality but is never anything other than consciousness, because the "thoughts" of divinity manifest as the "things" we perceive. We and the objects around us are in a sense separate from this ocean of consciousness, independent or "lesser" realities, and yet we and everything else besides exist in perfect unity in the One. Every aspect of this reality is mirrored in every other aspect, flowing out of and ultimately back into this divine source.

Paralleling the philosophy of India, Proclus wrote that the One is first known in two aspects, "being" and its "power." The similarity to Indian insights about Shiva (the ultimate being) and Shakti (Shiva's innate power) is worth noting.

Where does God fit into this picture? Those of us raised in the Judeo-Christian-Islamic tradition usually think of the creator god as the Supreme Being. But for Proclus (as for quite a few other teachers in his tradition, including Plato) the Creator, sometimes called the Demiurge or World Soul, is not identical with the One. Rather, our Maker, the intelligence of the cosmos, emanates out of pure being, which itself transcends the cyclic process of manifestation and dissolution. The Christian mystic Meister Eckhart would later also differentiate between the God who acts in the world and the Godhead who is beyond time, space, and causation.

The ultimate purpose of life, Proclus believed, is to return to the One, the very root of our being. But how? Like the yogis of India, Proclus taught that we must master the state of samadhi, transcendental consciousness, which Proclus called *henosis*. In this state the knower doesn't just think about an object, but through a supreme act of intuitive understanding actually becomes *one* with that object. Developing the intellect is only a preparatory exercise for learning to live in a state beyond the merely rational, an intuitive state of living unity with all things.

If this sounds abstract, try looking at it like Proclus did. Our senses tell us only about the small fraction of the total reality they're capable of perceiving. Our intellect, however, allows us to see the principles behind appearances, the $E=mc^2$ behind matter and energy, for example. At a still higher level, the level of intuition, we simply directly *know*. Proclus repeatedly made the point that in the end, the ultimate truth can't be grasped by our rational minds but only by cognizing it directly with our intuitive powers, merging into it through higher states of awareness like *henosis*. This is *exactly* what India's yogis teach even today.

Proclus was probably not familiar with Indian-style yoga. However, he did closely study the Chaldean system of spiritual practice, which operates on virtually identical principles as yoga. Chaldean art is filled with flowerlike images of the *sushumna* and the chakras, the nerve centers of the subtle body. When Proclus speaks of "the flower of the intellect" and "the flower of the soul" it's tempting to see veiled references to the *ajna chakra* and *sahasrara chakra*, centers of consciousness the Indian yoga masters also describe metaphorically as flowers. Proclus worked at length with symbols that connect human consciousness with subtle energies and higher realms of being, exactly as adepts in India still do. It was said that Proclus' command of inner forces became so fine tuned that he was able to control earthquakes and generate rain at will.

If Parmenides had been the closest Greece came to having its own great yogi-scholar Shankaracharya, Proclus was the Hellenistic world's Abhinava Gupta. Like the genius Kashmiri adept Abhinava Gupta, Proclus synthesized the work of the sages before him with absolutely dazzling brilliance and personally demonstrated mastery over higher states and subtle energies.

We yoga students can hardly resist asking whether Proclus could have attained enlightenment. According to his disciple and successor, Marinus, the answer is yes. Marinus tells us that Proclus purified himself through asceticism, virtue, service, intellectual inquiry, ritual, and meditation. "He rose above discursive reason and gained direct personal experience of the highest reality."

Today most scientists are not philosophers and most philosophers are not scientists. But many of the Greek sages explored both physics and metaphysics. Proclus was no exception. His scientific insights were astonishing for his time. He called attention to the fact that other planets have moons—a thousand years before Galileo. He claimed that the planets rotated on their axes and noted the existence of binary star systems. He understood that the planets travel in orbits in an era when even professional astronomers believed celestial bodies were attached to massive crystalline spheres. He wrote that seemingly empty space is in fact filled with invisible fields of energy. He even postulated the existence of subatomic particles.

## Breaking the Chain

Marinus tells us that one day Proclus received a panicked visit from Archiades, a prominent statesman who was one of his students. Archiades' only child was dying, and when all other efforts to save her failed, he turned to his guru to intercede on her behalf. Proclus left immediately for the temple of Asclepius, the Greek god of healing, to pray for the little girl. At the moment when Proclus finished his prayers, Archiades' daughter miraculously recovered. Then Marinus adds a comment of aching poignancy.

"At that time the temple of Asclepius was still standing, offering healing and comfort to the people, before it was destroyed by the Christians."

Proclus believed a man of true wisdom would never condemn anyone else's religion but should be "a priest of the universe," honoring all traditions. "It's not right to worship only in one temple. A truly spiritual man is a minister to all the faiths of the world." Proclus himself celebrated not only the Greek and Roman holy days but the Egyptian and Persian ones as well. He was convinced that the many gods worshiped in different religions were real, yet ultimately they were all manifestations of one Supreme Being.

Tragically, the atmosphere of religious tolerance and free inquiry the Greeks had long enjoyed was rapidly coming to an end. The Golden Chain of enlightened Western sages—with the living tradition of spiritual knowledge and practice it preserved—was about to be broken forever. Proclus was the last of his kind; not long after his death authorities closed the great Greek universities, burned their books, and drove their teachers out of Europe.

Proclus himself didn't live to see his beloved school demolished; he died in 485. (We're told he spent his last hours reciting the hymns of Orpheus.) But he surely saw the end coming. For a man who devoted his life to clearing a path to enlightenment for others, it must have been heartbreaking to foresee an era coming when that path would deliberately be blocked.

A new era that historians would later call the Dark Ages was rapidly descending on Europe. How could so much wisdom, the spiritual heritage of the Western world, be forgotten? We'll turn now to the last, sad days of the Hellenistic world.

# CHAPTER EIGHTEEN

# Extinguishing the Light

THE BEGINNING OF THE END of the ancient traditions, some said afterward, occurred in 415 C.E., when one of the best-loved spiritual teachers of Alexandria was brutally murdered.

Alexandria was the intellectual capital of the Western world, couched on the southeastern shore of the Mediterranean. Early in the third century B.C.E., Ptolemy I (the Greek general who ruled Egypt following Alexander the Great's untimely death) had chosen this city as the site of one of the greatest research centers ever created. Many of the leading scholars, scientists, and literary geniuses of the age gathered there to consolidate the collected knowledge of Western civilization in a great library. It contained hundreds of thousands of hand-copied books, the most important works of antiquity—many of them irreplaceable. Tragically, in 391 C.E. the Christian patriarch Theophilus, convinced that no books other than Christian scripture were worth reading, ordered the Library of Alexandria burned to the ground. It was one of the greatest crimes against humanity ever committed.

In an atmosphere increasingly hostile to intellectual activity and spiritual freedom, scholars such as Theon of Alexandria continued to write and teach. His specialties were astronomy and mathematics. But in both these fields his daughter Hypatia was said to outshine him. She had an impressive reputation as a scientist—give her a couple of days and she could build you an astrolabe to accurately measure the positions of the stars or a hydroscope to measure the weight of liquids for your chemistry experiments. But she was even better known as a Neoplatonist, a teacher like Proclus in the tradition of Plato and Plotinus. (Athens was still home to Plato's Academy, but it had other campuses, such as the school at Alexandria.) Her seminars were immensely popular, and we know from surviving reports by her students that they adored her. For her scholarship, scientific ability, and skill as an educator she was showered with awards.

Today we think of a professor as someone who gets up in a classroom and lectures, but many teachers in the Hellenistic era were more like traditional gurus in India. Often they taught out of their homes and regarded their students as virtual members of their family. For Neoplatonists like Hypatia, educating students intellectually was just one component of their training. Another was sitting together in silent meditation. Students were initiated in mental and spiritual disciplines so that they not only understood the higher realities Plato and Plotinus had spoken of intellectually but also experienced them directly in meditation. It was not enough to speak about the One; a true master had directly experienced the One, and a true student made every effort to do so too under her guidance. Hypatia was widely recognized as one of the great spiritual lights of her time, and would-be students vied to become her disciples.

Historical sources tell us that Cyril, the Bishop of Alexandria, was consumed with hatred for this great woman. He was an unpopular preacher who burned with jealousy as he watched crowds rush to hear Hypatia speak, while his own audiences remained small and unenthusiastic. But Cyril found a way to stir his congregation.

He convinced them Hypatia was a witch who used sorcery to captivate the crowds. She was a demonness from hell, he claimed, who committed unspeakable crimes such as "devotion to magic, astrolabes, and musical instruments."

Then it happened. In 415 C.E. a Christian mob, instigated by Cyril, attacked Hypatia in the street. Using whatever sharp objects they could find, even smashing jars to use the shards, they ripped her to pieces, tearing the very flesh off her bones. If the Greek tradition began with Orpheus being torn limb from limb, it ended ironically with Hypatia meeting the same grisly fate. Hypatia, like most of the Greek sages, is largely forgotten now, though the horror of her murder traumatized the Alexandrian academic community for more than a century. Today, however, the Roman Catholic Church hails Cyril as a saint.

In 380 C.E. the emperor Theodosius I declared Christianity to be the Roman state religion. A series of edicts ordered that the old Greek and Roman temples be destroyed. People barricaded themselves inside the temples, trying to save their sacred sites, but they were hacked to death or pulled out and crucified.

Many changes were imposed that were incomprehensible to non-Christians. Women were no longer allowed to teach, or even to practice medicine. People were not allowed to worship in their own way, even in their own homes. Annual festivals that had been celebrated for millennia were banned. The doctrine of reincarnation, once accepted by many Christians as having been taught by Christ himself, was anathematized. Incredibly, even vegetarianism was outlawed as an evil pagan practice. Throughout the empire books were confiscated and burned. Greek, the language of the educated for a thousand years, was replaced by Latin. Within a few generations it no longer mattered that a few Greek books survived in private collections; hardly anyone could read them anymore.

And then in 529 the Christian emperor Justinian ordered Plato's Academy in Athens closed forever. Thinking for oneself had literally become illegal. From then on the emperor and his advisors told the people what to believe.

Eight hundred years earlier Plato had spoken of a dark cave where people were held captive, unable to see anything but the play of shadows on the wall. Now, it appeared, absolutely no one would be allowed to leave the cave.

## What Happened?

The conflict between Christians and pagans can be traced back to 64 C.E., when a massive fire decimated a large section of the city of Rome. Many innocent people died in the flames, and thousands more were left homeless. Surprisingly, Emperor Nero claimed that Christians had started the fire. Christians were a small and obscure group at the time, far less known than many other religious cults, so it seems strange Nero would even have heard of them, much less have blamed them for this crime. However, not long before the fire some Christian zealots had been vocally condemning Rome as the modern "Babylon" and threatening that their God would destroy the city. When a deadly fire actually did break out, officials assumed the Christians were responsible.

After two thousand years it's impossible to say for sure who really started the fire, whether it was Nero himself, as most people believe today; whether it was a mob of religious extremists, as Nero claimed; or for that matter whether it was simply a cow knocking over a lantern. But the initial perception seems to have been that Christians were the culprits and that their cult was extremist and dangerous.

Ironically, it appears that the Romans responded to early Christians in much the same way as many Americans reacted to Muslims after Islamic fanatics attacked the World Trade Center

on September 11, 2001. Christians were now seen as potential ter-
rorists. Some of them were rounded up and thrown to the lions, a
common and unbelievably gruesome method of execution in those
brutal days. Later pagan emperors, still suspicious but attempting
to be more humane, offered to release Christian prisoners who
demonstrated they weren't anti-Rome by swearing allegiance
to the state and the state gods. This was unthinkable to many
Christians, who bowed only to their own deity. And so mistrust
between the two groups continued to grow.

Another source of contention was that Christians believed
their faith was completely unique. In the Christian view, Jesus'
incarnation on Earth was a one-time-only personal intervention
by God. Many pagans felt uneasy with these claims. Their perspective was that many virgin-born "sons of God," such as Hercules,
had appeared in the past. They noted that the Christians' sacred
rite of Holy Communion was unmistakably patterned on Orphic
ritual; the cult of the Virgin Mother was incorporated into Christianity directly from the Egyptian Isis religion; the doctrine of a
risen savior had been brought over from Mithraism; and the idea
of a battle against Satan and a final day of judgment were obviously borrowed from Zoroastrianism. Jesus had no doubt been a
great teacher and healer, they felt, but so were numerous pagan
saints, such as Apollonius of Tyana. Just as Jesus appeared to
have risen from the dead, so had Apollonius when he appeared to
Emperor Aurelian to save the city of Tyana from Lucian's attack.

Most puzzling of all to the pagans was how all their ancestors, many of whom had served the gods devotedly, could be
condemned to eternal hell because they hadn't accepted Christ
as their savior. After all, they'd never heard of him—he hadn't
even been born yet. The Christians' insistence that everyone
else in the world must immediately abandon their own faiths and

accept Jesus in order to avoid hellfire just didn't make sense to most pagans.

Christians passionately believed there was only one God, and that respect for many different gods was deeply wrong. This confused pagan observers, who thought the Christians worshiped a number of different gods themselves, including a Father, Son, and Holy Ghost. Many pagan sages had also emphasized that there was only one God, but they were comfortable with people calling that supreme deity by familiar names like Zeus, Jupiter, or Magna Mater ("Great Mother"). They believed in allowing people to worship in their traditional manner, provided their practices didn't break the law.

Christians, on the other hand, sincerely believed that only their religion was acceptable to God and that it was their duty to share the good news of Jesus' self-sacrifice with everyone else. They quickly developed an increasingly large and close-knit community that especially embraced the poor and uneducated on the margins of Roman society. They taught that Christ's death and resurrection had automatically made salvation available to anyone who believed the same as they did. This was in some ways a much easier path than the older Greek traditions, where teachers like Iamblichus and Proclus insisted that in order to free yourself from the wheel of rebirth, you had to do your own spiritual homework. In Christianity, Jesus had done it for you.

## Against the Christians

It's thought provoking to read the response of the Hellenistic masters to Christian claims. In his book *Against the Christians*, Porphyry went through the Gospels passage by passage, raising a host of objections. For example, if only those with faith can enter heaven, and Jesus says anyone with even a mustard seed worth of faith can move mountains merely by giving a command, but the highest Christian bishop can't even move a hairpin simply by commanding it, then clearly no one has the faith Jesus demands, so no one is going to heaven.

Some of Porphyry's numerous other objections were less facile. He pointed out that Jesus suffered terribly in the Garden of Gethsemane and later on the cross, frightened and despairing. Yet common Roman soldiers faced their deaths with more faith and courage. Macarius, the Christian theologian who answered Porphyry's criticisms, said Jesus was only pretending to be afraid in order to "tease" Satan.

Porphyry, who was Syrian, knew the region around the Sea of Galilee well. He pointed out that it was, in reality, a small lake in which, as any sailor can tell you, waves large enough to engulf a boat simply can't form. Yet Christian scriptures describe a ferocious storm in which the disciples' boat was in such danger, Jesus had to still the waves. Macarius' answer is fascinating. He said the story was only allegorical. The stormy sea represented "the brine and gall of human existence" and Jesus' action symbolized his power over the devil. When I was taught the story of Jesus stilling the sea in Sunday school, no one mentioned the story was just an allegory.

In his *Enneads*, Plotinus also expressed his reservations about Christianity as it was being taught in Rome at that time. "They say look to God, without offering any instruction how to do so. Some believe that merely by remembering God's name they will be saved, and neglect the purification of their souls. Without spiritual self-discipline, *God* is only a word."

By the fifth century, when Proclus was teaching in Athens, the western Roman Empire was in turmoil. The Huns were a continual threat, illegal immigrants poured over the borders, and the Visigoths sacked Rome in 410. The Roman legions, who had maintained national security for centuries, could no longer protect even their own capital. In addition, Roman culture had become quite decadent and corrupt; in fact numerous parallels between Rome at that time and present-day America are extremely unsettling.

Starting with Constantine, who became emperor in 306, many Roman emperors adopted Christianity, though sad to say, their reigns were seldom less brutal than those of the pagan rulers. But their active hostility toward non-Christian temples and teachers left the pagan population shell-shocked, like the Native Americans after European settlers systematically set out to annihilate their culture.

One law after another was passed against followers of the old wisdom tradition. One school after another was shut down. One library after another was committed to flames. Over the years, household by household, ancient beliefs were eradicated. Europe was slowly Christianized, and the contributions of the Hellenistic masters—the light of Western civilization—were gradually forgotten.

## Returning to Jesus

Today we consider meditation, reincarnation, vegetarianism, spiritual practices designed to turn us inward, and a recognition of the essential unity of all things to be purely Eastern. We've forgotten that these teachings were once an integral part of our own Western spiritual heritage.

Then in 1945 an amazing discovery in the chalk cliffs near Nag Hammadi, Egypt, riveted the world's attention. There scholars found very early Christian texts, some as old as the books of the New Testament, that cast astonishing new light on Jesus' teaching. These manuscripts had been written long before Constantine became the first Christian emperor of Rome, in fact long before the theological conferences that coined the doctrines we think of as Christianity today. And yet rather than rushing to publish these exciting new texts, Church leaders dragged their feet for decade after decade, denying the public—and even other scholars—access to this material. A whole generation of Christians lived and died without learning what these vitally important manuscripts had to tell us about Jesus and his mission.

Today this treasure trove is finally available in English, though its publication came with amazingly little fanfare, as if authorities didn't really want people to know about it. Christians in most churches never hear their pastors or priests even obliquely refer to these manuscripts, even though they're probably the most important works about early Christianity other than the Bible itself.

*Why?*

Could it be because these manuscripts prove that the earliest generations of Christians were avid readers of Plato and the *Corpus Hermetica?* (The early Christian community at Nag Hammadi had carefully preserved Platonic and Hermetic writings, along with Christian texts.) Could it be because these manuscripts explain that not only Jesus but also the prophets of other cultures—such as Orpheus and Zoroaster—had been sent by God to lead humanity to salvation? Could it be because they acknowledge not only the fatherhood but also the motherhood of the Supreme Being (in fact they're full of references to the Goddess), and call on women to play a major role in the Church? Perhaps it's because they insist that the real resurrection is not the resurrection of the dead body but of the living soul from the tomb of its body—that heaven doesn't consist of life in a reanimated physical body but in a body of pure light.

In a Nag Hammadi text, the disciple Matthew asks Jesus to show him heaven. Jesus answers, "Every one of you who has known himself has already seen it. For the consciousness that asks the question is itself the answer." Jesus urging us to know our Inner Self? They didn't teach that in my Sunday school either!

"Where will we go after we die?" the disciples ask Jesus. "As far as you can reach," the master replies. Jesus repeatedly explains that the soul existed before it was born in a physical body, and that if it doesn't find the light in this life, it will have to "be born again" in yet another body.

Jesus tells his disciple James, "You must free yourself from the blind idea that you are your body. Then you will reach 'The One Who Is.' At that point you will no longer be James. You will be 'The One Who Is.' " Apparently, when the twentieth-century Hindu sage Ramana Maharshi challenged his devotees to ask "Who am I?" and uncover their true identity in spirit, he was unwittingly echoing Christ's advice.

Jesus continually urged his followers to meditate on the inner reality, explaining that it is their mastery of higher states of consciousness that will save them from the round of death and rebirth, allowing them to travel in higher worlds as far as they can reach. Throughout the early Christian era, the Desert Fathers in Egypt followed Jesus' instructions to practice strict self-discipline and meditation.

These texts raise a sobering question. Is it possible that in their enthusiasm to rid the world of all spiritual traditions except their own, overzealous Christians may have inadvertently also eradicated many of Jesus' own teachings? I'm forcibly struck by the fact that some of these very early Christian texts are closer in spirit to the writings of the Greek sages, and definitely closer to the teachings I learned in my yoga and meditation classes, than they are to the modern Christian doctrine I learned as a child.

The poet T. S. Eliot wrote movingly of returning to the point from which we started our journey, and truly seeing it for the first time. I was raised a Christian but wandered from the fold because there were aspects of my tradition that didn't make sense to me. Having absorbed the spiritual insights of both the Eastern spiritual masters and our own early Western sages, I feel as though I'm now seeing Jesus with fresh eyes. I read his words for the hundredth time, but for the first time I feel as though I understand them. Jesus taught within the context of the Hellenistic world, and to understand that world is to understand Christ that much better.

The yogis in India often use the phrase *Sanatana Dharma*. It means "the eternal tradition." A thousand years ago the great Muslim scholar Al-Biruni (who studied in India for thirteen years) wrote that although the great religions, Christianity, Islam, Judaism, and Hinduism, all appear very different externally, their mystical inner cores are remarkably similar. They all seem to share the same heart.

You can turn away from "the eternal tradition," but it just won't go away. You can turn your back on the Sun, but it won't stop shining. Why is it that when we hear the words of the ancient masters, Eastern or Western, they resonate so deeply with us? Is it because Plato was right when he said the soul *remembers* the truth when it hears it again?

The spiritual masters of the ancient Western world were servants of the eternal tradition. It's amazing what we can learn from these great teachers when we pause, even for just a moment, to *listen*.

## Reclaiming the Past

I believe it's time to resurrect the ancient sages of the Western world, to once again consider what these masters had to say about the nature of the cosmos and the nature of consciousness. When we look to these great men and women, we discover that the gulf between East and West is not nearly as wide as we had imagined.

East and West share a common inner tradition. Those of us who've had the good fortune to study in the yogic lineages of India have discovered a brimming spring of spiritual knowledge and practices closely related to that of our spiritual ancestors in Europe. It tastes like the "living waters" Jesus urged his disciples to drink.

The rediscovery of the Hellenistic masters in the late 1400s ended the European Dark Ages and ignited the Renaissance. But under the onslaught of scientific materialism, this fountain of inspiration was once again turned off. The works of the masters grew dusty on neglected library shelves. We no longer realized—or even cared—how much our ancestors had to say to us. No doubt this is why when my generation was introduced to yoga and meditation in the 1960s, it felt like stumbling on a lush oasis in a desert wasteland. We were *starving* for spiritual sustenance, for the "bread of life" Jesus had promised. Jesus complained about the priests in his own time, "You hold the keys to the kingdom of heaven, but you won't let anyone in. And you won't go in yourselves!" Sometimes it seems as though the priests of our own time are no different.

The sages of both East and West were human conduits for a perennial tradition that gives spiritual value to our lives, leading us from ignorance to fuller understanding, from darkness to light, and from the perishable to the imperishable. Perhaps it's time to return to Delphi, to revisit Athens, to rebuild the shattered shrines of Tyana. Perhaps it's finally time for those of us born in the West to reclaim our lost spiritual masters.

# CHAPTER NINETEEN

# The India Connection

SO WHERE DOES ALL THIS leave us now? Can we children of the West reconnect with our lost Hellenistic heritage? Even if it were possible after all these years, why bother?

Suppose your grandfather owned a treasure, a golden chalice worth millions of dollars. Your father, though, thought the cup was worthless. He packed it away and eventually forgot all about it. If by chance you happened to find it, wouldn't you be delighted? And what is the Holy Grail but the cup of wisdom, anyway? Much has been lost of the treasure our Graeco-Roman forebears intended for us, but at least some of their enormous spiritual wealth can be salvaged from the sea of time.

What is gone, sadly, is lost irretrievably. With rare exceptions, such as the remarkable visualization exercise Plotinus described in his *Enneads*, we don't know the specific spiritual practices the Greeks used. We know they existed—Greek authors frequently refer to them—but the details are gone forever. The Greeks just didn't write them down.

Why not?

As usual, Plato has the answer, which appears in a conversation he jotted down between his guru Socrates and an acquaintance named Phaedrus:

"There's an Egyptian god named Thoth," Socrates began, "who first invented mathematics, geometry, and astronomy, as well as games like checkers and gambling. But he's especially famous for his most important invention of all, writing. Thoth introduced these great advances to Ammon, who was king of Egypt at the time. Thoth was particularly proud of writing, which he believed would greatly benefit the Egyptians, making them wiser and greatly expanding what they'd be able to remember.

"But Ammon was unimpressed. He said, 'No, Thoth, just the opposite is true: writing will weaken, not strengthen, the memory. People will no longer exercise their memory once they put their trust in the written word. Why should they memorize a subject when it's written down and they can refer to a piece of paper any time they need to? They'll lose their wisdom when they no longer deeply assimilate what they've been taught by memorizing it. You haven't invented a tool for remembering but for reminding, which will give people only the appearance of wisdom. They'll think they know everything when in fact they know next to nothing at all.'"

Socrates continued, "A written page is much like a painting. The figures in a painting look as though they're alive, but if you ask them anything, they'll just stand there silently. It's the same thing with a book. If you have questions about what you've just read, the book can't answer you. If you have criticisms about the material, it can't defend itself. What's more, once something's been written down it's available to anyone who happens to read it, whether or not they have any business with the information, and whether or not they have any aptitude for the material."

Socrates was making the point that knowledge of real value comes through the guru-disciple relationship. "Living instruction directly from a person who knows the subject" is vastly superior to the written word. Now, there's some irony in the fact that Plato was the one writing this, especially since Plato is the author of thousands of pages himself. But written information was always meant to be generously supplemented with personal instruction from a qualified teacher. Spiritual practices in particular, both in Greece and India, were rarely committed to writing in more than a terse or veiled manner. Real spiritual training came through the oral tradition. True understanding could be passed only from one mind directly to another. Consciousness itself, not paper, was the only fitting medium for wisdom.

How can we ever retrieve the long-lost spiritual practices of the Western wisdom tradition? We can't. But we can do the next best thing: turn to a related tradition that didn't suffer the same setbacks Greece did, where the knowledge of the ancients is still alive and sages are still honored. The yoga tradition survived every natural and man-made catastrophe visited on India. And when we read the Greeks with India in mind, suddenly the old texts spring to life. Let me give you six very brief examples (out of hundreds) of how the living tradition of the East brings the nearly extinct tradition of the West back to life.

## Angels

Today scholars are puzzled by numerous statements by Plato that his master, Socrates, had a "spirit guide." That sounds bizarre to modern Western scholars who like to think of Socrates as the preeminent champion of logic. Yet millions of Indians are still routinely initiated into working with an inner guide. A "guardian angel" that a Hindu feels especially close to, worships daily, and draws inspiration, strength, protection, and intuitive information from is called an *ishta devata* (literally, "personal deity"). Many Hindus chant the mantra of their *devata* every day of their lives.

Musicians and writers are inspired to compose by their *ishta devatas*; teachers find the right words to explain a subject, and meditators reach higher states of awareness—all with the help of this inner muse. It's understood as a real entity that exists outside oneself yet simultaneously as a higher manifestation of one's own Inner Self. In India, inner and outer worlds are not regimented into two distinct compartments but are seen as overlapping, integrated, and ultimately identical dimensions.

## Cosmology

Sages like Proclus spoke of higher realms in which consciousness and energy were only beginning to separate out from each other into the mental and physical worlds we all know. While Proclus and his predecessors approached this topic from a different angle than the Indians, their conclusions are remarkably reminiscent of the first five levels of manifestation delineated by India's northern Shaivites. This is the "Big Bang theory" of the yogis, only in the Indian version consciousness is present from the very first instant.

If you sit down and read Proclus from a Western perspective, his devotion to these seemingly abstract higher realities is difficult to understand. If you've been trained in a tradition like Shaivism, however, you'll appreciate that these inner realities are actually experienced in deep states of meditation. They're not just abstruse concepts but are real experiences accessible to one with expanded awareness. To Proclus, as to yogis still today, understanding these states was tantamount to peering into the mind of God. Divine intelligence wasn't sealed away in heaven but was accessible to human awareness through superconscious states.

## Superconsciousness

The later Greek tradition concerned itself with *henosis*, a state of consciousness in which an individual knows an object (perhaps even God) by merging with it completely. It's derived from the

Greek word *hen* (pronounced "hane"), which means "unity," as does the Sanskrit word *yoga*. The fact that *henosis* was a real state, actually achievable with intense focus and lots of practice, seems to have been lost on Western scholars. Yet the yoga tradition even today offers a graded series of mental exercises to help people attain this state, called samadhi in Sanskrit. Saints and advanced yogis can still be seen sitting in samadhi—or *henosis*—today.

I've had the opportunity to watch such modern sages as Swami Rama of the Himalayas, Shree Maa of Kamakhya, and Ammachi of Amritapuri in this illumined state. The degree of insight and healing power they bring from that level of inner being out into our workaday world is truly phenomenal. No wonder the Greeks valued this state so highly.

## Spiritual Practice

As Rome consolidated its hold on the Western world, its soldiers carried Mithraism with them throughout the European continent. It's a dead tradition now; scholars can only guess what the followers of this great system, which once rivaled Christianity, practiced and believed. A controversial papyrus called the "Mithraic Ritual," dated to the early fourth century, may offer important clues.

In this internal ritual, the aspirant begins by lifting his awareness through the five elements, (earth, water, fire, air, ether) along a "pipe" at the top of which lies a "golden disk." Yoga students will immediately recognize the practice of *bhuta shuddhi*, or "cleansing of the elements," associated with the chakras or centers of consciousness along the spine. Even breathing exercises (Sanskrit *pranayama*) are included in the Mithraic meditation, just as in the form of *bhuta shuddhi* practiced in India. The Mithraic practice culminates in entering the golden disk, a technique called *bindu bhedana* in Sanskrit. If this is an authentic Mithraic rite, Roman soldiers were practicing advanced yogic techniques! Considering that when they got up in the morning they didn't know whether they'd still be alive at the end of the day, there could well have been serious interest in spirituality among many of the troops.

Mithraism appears to have much in common with the astral religion of the *Rig Veda*, India's earliest-surviving religious document. Mitra is one of the names of the Sun in the *Rig Veda*. (*Mitra* was pronounced "Mithra" in Persia and Rome.) Both Mithraism and the *Veda* focus on the stars of the ecliptic, celestial equator, and north celestial pole, understood as external projections of inner points of light (*bindus*) experienced in meditation.

## Archetypes

Plato is especially famous for the concept of archetypes, patterns that exist in the mental universe, or Cosmic Mind. These form the framework over which the physical universe is woven. Everything in the outer world bears the stamp of these inner realities and shows divine intelligence at work. This is of course the opposite of the modern scientific view, which claims that intelligence arises—entirely by chance—out of matter. Plato says, on the contrary, that when consciousness impresses itself on matter, chaos is transformed into cosmos, order emerges from entropy, and lifeless rock becomes living, organic matter.

This paradigm, derided as obsolete by scientists today, is still very much alive in the East. To this day yogis say that when *purusha*, divine intelligence, directs *prakriti*, or unorganized matter, then matter comes alive, becomes ensouled, and out of cosmic dust form living worlds and the individual beings who inhabit them.

We can see these principles at work in the biological sciences today. The DNA in an acorn, for example, contains the "idea" or archetypal pattern of an oak tree and purposefully directs the air and soil and water around it, shaping them into a magnificent tree. The hallmark of intelligence is that it is creative. The eastern view is that matter has no creative potency of its own but is the outer substance that the living forces of the inner world mold to create a universe in which souls can play.

This is not a trivial point. For yogis, the purpose of meditating on a mantra is to connect with the living energy *behind* the sound. Elaborate visualizations are also used in both the Hindu and Buddhist traditions to gain access to the living fields of energy depicted in paintings of deities or in yantras and mandalas. These fields of intelligence, called *devatas,* make up the inner world and control the outer world. In their meditative practice, yogis still work with "archetypes" something like those Plato wrote about centuries ago.

## The Good

Perhaps the most common term that Plato and Plotinus used in referring to the Supreme Reality was "the Good." Curiously, this is a direct translation of one of the most common Sanskrit names for the Supreme Reality, "Shiva."

And so ironically, just as Columbus sailed west to reach the East, today we find ourselves heading east to reach the West. Clues to a deeper understanding of the Hellenistic tradition lie in its sister tradition in India. In many ways Hindus maintaining their traditional philosophical and spiritual traditions today are closer to the ancient Greeks than the Greeks' own living descendants.

## The Unbroken Tradition

Till only very recently, modern Western scholars have been in near-complete denial about the parallels between the ancient Greek and Indian philosophical traditions. But why should these similarities surprise us? Some of them may be a result of shared cultural roots deep in Indo-European antiquity. After all, the Graeco-Romans and North Indians speak related languages and have numbers of deities in common such as Jupiter/Dyaus Pitar and Uranus/Varuna. Most north Indians and most Europeans descend from the same legendary forefather, named Manu in India. That's why we English speakers call ourselves mankind, which literally means "children of Manu."

Scholars also have the false impression that ancient Greece and India were immeasurably far apart. We forget that even in antiquity these regions were linked by the Near Eastern civilizations in between them, such as the Assyrians and Chaldeans, and later the Persians. Trade between these regions has been going on for at least five thousand years; couldn't ideas as well as merchandise have crossed borders? Given that certain popular myths, such as the Great Flood and the Garden of Eden, were shared by cultures as far separated as northern Europe and Bengal, it's possible we're not giving the ancients enough credit for having developed a true world culture—or for preserving a still more ancient tradition that originated far back in human prehistory, when our distant ancestors split into separate cultures.

But to claim, as some scholars have, that all ideas the ancient Greeks and Indians have in common were brought to India by Alexander the Great skirts a very substantial problem: most of those ideas had been kicking around in India for centuries, sometimes millennia, before Alexander arrived. Western scholars— who idolized the Greeks—were anxious to avoid the possible implication that the influence might have flowed not from Greece to India but from India to Greece.

One effective way to avoid this conclusion was simply to rewrite Indian history. The *Veda*, the oldest text of Hindu philosophy and spirituality, had been compiled in northwestern India sometime before 3100 B.C.E., according to the Indians themselves. Astronomical references and descriptions of geological terrain in the *Veda* confirm the traditional dating. Max Müller, a nineteenth-century German scholar of impeccable credentials, simply moved the date forward to 1200 B.C.E. This meant that Indian history had to be radically compressed to accommodate *two thousand missing years*. Major historical figures such as Buddha and the great Hindu yogi-philosopher Shankaracharya were reassigned to dates centuries later than their own lineages had recorded. These incorrect dates made fair comparisons between Indian and Greek thinkers impossible, seriously confusing the issue of mutual influence. But the claim that the Greeks were the first philosophers and scientists was now secure. If India had impressive philosophical, medical, or scientific systems, it must be because they'd been imported from Greece!

Toward the end of his life Müller emphasized that he'd just been guessing when he suggested the *Veda* was composed in 1200 B.C.E., and for all he knew it "could have been composed in 15,000 B.C.E." But the damage had been done. India, a vastly older and far more sophisticated culture, with an unbroken tradition of intellectual excellence and spiritual preeminence going back to the fourth millennium B.C.E. at the latest, was now portrayed as an intellectual backwater. Greece, a young culture with a shattered history, was elevated to a vastly exaggerated role in the development of human civilization. The Greeks were credited with discovering the precession of the equinoxes, for example, and the Pythagorean theorem. These "breakthroughs" were already old news in India. The Greeks were even credited with inventing democracy. Democratic *sanghams* had been part of the Indian political landscape for centuries before the Greeks ever dreamed of experimenting with representative government.

But I don't want to overstate my point. If the similarities

between the ancient Greek and Indian traditions are striking, the differences are even more so. The Hellenistic world had its saints and sages, tantrics and ascetics. But these men and women were comparatively rare. When Christianity rose to prominence, it destroyed the older wisdom tradition with comparative ease. In India saints and sages have always been astonishingly common. Probably no other culture in human history has fostered so many truly great spiritual adepts century after century. When Islam entered India around 1000 C.E., it periodically attempted to exterminate India's age-old mystical tradition. It made very little headway. No matter how many temples Muslim zealots destroyed, they couldn't kill all the yogis and swamis, India's living temples of spirit. No matter how many libraries they burned, they couldn't kill all the brahmins, who had memorized their voluminous sacred literature and were in fact human books.

A thousand years of attacks and foreign occupation took their toll on India, and gradually it was reduced to the state of poverty and corruption we see today. People forget that for most of its history, going back at the very least to the Indus civilization of 2600 B.C.E., India led the world in prosperity, urban development, science, mathematics, literature, and spirituality. The Greeks, it is true, created a great civilization. But they freely acknowledged their debt to older, wiser cultures, a fact nineteenth- and twentieth-century Western scholars preferred to ignore.

I love and respect the ancient Greek sages, but if I had to choose only one spiritual tradition to study, I would choose India's. The Indian tradition remains unbroken. The yoga lineages are still alive, and techniques for translating intellectual knowledge into living experience are still taught there. Enlightened masters aren't just inspiring legends; you can still find Self-realized saints in India. But, thank God, we don't have to choose between the two traditions—we can, if we wish, learn from them both.

Perhaps with the help of Eastern insight we can forge anew the Golden Chain that was broken when the ancient Graeco-Roman academies were closed. Extinguished fires can be relit. In these dark, intolerant times, that ancient light could illuminate the world.

CHAPTER TWENTY

# Exploring Our Western Heritage

If these chapters have whetted your appetite to learn more about our Western heritage, as I hope they have, where can you turn for more information?

I want to encourage you to pick up copies of Plotinus' *Enneads* and the *Corpus Hermetica*, perhaps the two most exciting and inspiring books on the inner tradition ever produced in the West. But friends who've followed my advice have complained they couldn't understand even the first few paragraphs. There are two major problems in approaching the works of our Western spiritual elders. First, many of them wrote in technical philosophical language we're no longer familiar with. Second and far worse, the majority of translators are scholars who translate for other scholars, not for the general public. They don't even try to make the ancient Greek classics accessible to a novice reader.

So what can you do if you want to learn more about our Hellenistic heritage, but you don't feel up to tackling confusing Greek jargon? Here are some entry-level books beginners can handle.

CHAPTER ONE—The Light of the West

*Lives of Eminent Philosophers* by Diogenes Laërtes, translated by R. D. Hicks, two volumes. This entertaining book by a third-century C.E. historian covers many of the most important sages and philosophers of the Greek tradition. It includes lively gossip about the great thinkers of antiquity and brief summaries of their teachings.

CHAPTER TWO—The Mystery Religions

You can read about the discovery of the Oracle of the Dead by the man who found it in *In the Footsteps of Orpheus* by R. F. Paget. For color photographs of this amazing site (surely one of the most astonishing archaeological finds in the world) and more up-to-date information, pick up *Netherworld* by Robert Temple.

The best book on Greek oracles in general is the wonderful *Have You Been to Delphi?* by Roger Lipsey. I highly recommend this charming book, which explains how the Greeks sought guidance from higher dimensions of reality. The book is full of delightful stories of living Hellenic spirituality.

CHAPTER THREE—Calming the Savage Heart

*The Hymns of Orpheus* by R. C. Hogart is probably the most accessible introduction to the Orphic tradition.

CHAPTER FOUR—Helen's Chalice

*The Presocratic Philosophers* by G. S. Kirk, J. E. Raven, and M. Schofield introduces you to the words of the ancient thinkers themselves. Be prepared for a worldview very different from your own.

Note that from the eighteenth through the twentieth centuries, dubious ideas about "the Greek miracle" went unquestioned in American and European universities. This view seriously proposed that the Greeks were the only ancient people capable of thinking logically and that they alone gave rise to the brilliance of later European civilization. That is to say, almost all the great advances in science, technology, and commerce in history were generated by white European males! (You will no doubt be astonished to learn that this idea was conceived and promoted by white European males.)

In the twenty-first century, new research, alert to the illusions born of racial and ethnic bias, has begun producing a far more balanced view of history that acknowledges the massive contributions of other cultures and the astonishing extent of their influence on European development. See, for example, *The Eastern Origins of Western Civilisation* by John M. Hobson. For a whole new perspective on the breathtaking achievements of Native American cultures, which far surpassed that of their European contemporaries in some respects, see Charles C. Mann's *1491: New Revelations of the Americas Before Columbus*.

CHAPTER FIVE—The Spiritual Colony

*The Pythagorean Sourcebook and Library,* translated by Kenneth S. Guthrie, is the ideal place to begin if you're interested in learning more about Pythagoras.

CHAPTER SIX—The Road to Reality

Scholar Peter Kingsley has been doing groundbreaking research on the major Greek sages before Socrates. His books *In the Dark Places of Wisdom* and *Reality* are outstanding—and fortunately also very readable—introductions to Parmenides.

CHAPTER SEVEN—The Private Investigator

Only scraps of Heraclitus' writings have survived. For a glimpse of this influential figure, you might refer to *Heraclitus: Fragments,* translated by T. M. Robinson.

CHAPTER EIGHT—The Man Who Stopped the Wind

Peter Kingsley's book *Ancient Philosophy, Mystery, and Magic* is intermediate-level reading. I call it to your attention because it addresses important aspects of spirituality in Empedocles, which most Western scholars before Kingsley ignored. If you're ready for an intellectual adventure, this book will take your breath away.

CHAPTER NINE—Atoms and the Void

It's pitiful how little of Democritus' huge body of work has survived. But *On the Nature of the Universe* by Lucretius, translated by R. E. Latham, is a good example of an important early work influenced by Democritus and Epicurus. Lucretius lived around 100–55 B.C.E.

CHAPTER TEN—The Man Who Lost a Continent

If you'd like to get a taste of Plato, I'd recommend that you begin with three of his dialogues: *Timaeus, Critias,* and *Phaedo.* The first two introduce the legend of Atlantis and many of Plato's other interesting views and speculations as well. The *Phaedo,* which tells the story of Socrates' last hours on Earth, is one of the greatest works in the whole of Western literature. I use *Plato: Complete Works*, edited by John M. Cooper. However, a more affordable option might be any of the numerous excellent translations of individual texts by Plato.

CHAPTER ELEVEN—The Master of Those Who Know

Of the Greek philosophers, Aristotle may be the toughest to read. His works don't survive in thoughtfully crafted essays but in incomplete notes that either he or his students jotted down. Ease yourself gently into the work of this ancient genius with John A. Vella's *Aristotle: A Guide for the Perplexed.*

CHAPTER TWELVE—Apollonius Was Like the Sun

For information about Apollonius, your best bet is to go straight to the primary source: *The Life of Apollonius of Tyana* by Philostratus, translated by F. C. Conybeare, two volumes. It's flabbergasting to me that more people aren't familiar with this material. Apollonius was one of the most dynamic personalities of early Western history. The account of his stay with an enclave of yogis in northern India is fascinating and historically important.

CHAPTER THIRTEEN—The Priest of Delphi

Plutarch is one of the most readable of the ancients. Sitting down with one of his books is like listening to your favorite uncle tell stories. You might enjoy the biographies of great Greek and Roman figures Plutarch compiled in his *Lives* (various translators). I particularly enjoyed his *Moralia,* which contains his views on important religious and moral issues, such as animal rights and the dignity of women.

CHAPTER FOURTEEN—From the Alone to the Alone

All of ancient Greek thought culminated in Plotinus, and no thinker since in the Western world has matched his majesty of vision. In my opinion, Plotinus is as good as it gets. The two best beginning-level entry ports are *Return to the One* by Brian Hines and *Plotinus or the Simplicity of Vision* by Pierre Hadot (translated by Michael Chase), though even these marvelous books barely begin to do justice to the great master's insights.

When you feel ready for Plotinus himself, two good English translations of the *Enneads* are available, one by A. H. Armstrong, in seven volumes, the other by Stephen MacKenna. Be forewarned: the *Enneads* are not light reading, and it may take you a few chapters to get used to the Greek vocabulary. Don't confuse this masterpiece with *The Aeneid* by Virgil!

CHAPTER FIFTEEN—The Work of Enlightenment

*Theurgy and the Soul* by Gregory Shaw is an amazingly excellent introduction to the life and teaching of Iamblichus. Anyone interested in the science behind ritual magic and divination will find a treasure trove of insight here.

CHAPTER SIXTEEN—The Shepherd of Men

There are a number of translations of the *Corpus Hermetica,* each with its strengths and weaknesses. You might try, to start out, *Hermetica: The Greek Corpus Hermeticum and the Latin Asclepius,* translated by Brian P. Copenhaver. *The Way of Hermes* by Clement Salaman, et al, is also satisfying. Modern "occult" and "channeled" works pale before the spiritual sublimity of this all-time Egyptian classic.

CHAPTER SEVENTEEN—The Golden Chain

*The Life of Proclus* by Marinus, translated by Thomas Taylor, is probably the most easily digestible introduction to Proclus, though it's all too short. If you're willing to dive deeper into the amazing thought world of Proclus and aren't afraid of more intermediate-level material, I highly recommend the superb study *Proclus: Neo-Platonic Philosophy and Science* by Lucas Siorvanes.

CHAPTER EIGHTEEN—Extinguishing the Light

*Hypatia of Alexandria* by Maria Dzielska is a fine study of one of the great women sages of Western antiquity. Disappointingly, female masters have generally been poorly documented in the West. For an introduction to the information that has survived, check out the first volume of *A History of Women Philosophers,* edited by Mary Ellen Waithe.

*The Gnostic Gospels* by Elaine Pagels is one of numerous good introductions to aspects of the original Christian tradition that were suppressed along with pagan spirituality. *The Nag Hammadi Library* itself is edited by James Robinson and will change your understanding of early Christianity forever. However, if you do not already have some background knowledge of the so-called heretical traditions, you will find it tough reading.

Those of us raised in the Christian tradition have learned about the rise of Christianity from the perspective of our own faith. A number of eye-opening books review this phase of Western history from a non-Christian point of view. *Porphyry's Against the Christians*, edited and translated by R. Joseph Hoffmann, summarizes the pagan response to the Gospels. It's fascinating and very surprising. *The Emperor Julian* by Constance Head is the most readable introduction to the brilliant Roman emperor who saw the Dark Ages coming and tried to prevent them. It's the poignant true story of a thoughtful and compassionate man taking a stand against the flow of history.

CHAPTER NINETEEN—The India Connection

A recent study, *The Shape of Ancient Thought* by Thomas McEvilley of Rice University, finally spells out the obvious: the Greek and Indian philosophical traditions are related. Even at 732 pages the study barely scrapes the surface of this vast topic. One caveat: McEvilley still subscribes to a version of early Indian history that has recently been discredited by archaeologists. Also take the dates he offers for early Indian historical figures with a grain of salt.

CHAPTER TWENTY—Exploring Our Western Heritage

There are two other beginning-level books I'd suggest you have a look at. The first, *Enchiridion* (Greek for "handbook"), was written by a slave named Epictetus who was born around 55 C.E. He was eventually freed by his owner and spent the rest of his life teaching philosophy in Rome. This short manual on living serenely in tough times is a classic of Stoic philosophy.

The second book, *The Consolation of Philosophy* by Boethius, (translated by Richard Green) is widely considered the last great classic of the Hellenistic world. The fact that it was composed in Latin, not Greek, was a sign of the new Christian era beginning to dominate Europe. It was written in 524 C.E. as the author sat in prison awaiting execution. Boethius was an honest government officer who'd been framed by corrupt politicians who feared he would expose them. In this deeply moving work, the author grapples with the age-old question of why bad things happen to good people and asks himself if he'd have been better off lying and taking bribes like everyone else. After all, in that case he would have lived to a ripe old age! This fantastically inspiring work was one of the best-loved books in Western Europe for a thousand years and is still well worth reading today.

## Learning More

If you have trouble ordering any of the books in this list, remember one of the most valuable resources available to modern humanity: the public library. Your local librarian would be happy to help you track down the volumes you want.

Because the book you're holding in your hands is a very general introduction, I've left out far more than I've squeezed in. Important teachers such as Zeno of Elea and Zeno of Citium are missing. Sometimes I've simplified complex Greek doctrines to an extent that would make a scholar blanch. I've also avoided splicing in many technical issues that readers who want to know more about the Greeks will need to consider. Virtually every aspect of the Greek material is controversial, from which of the colorful stories about the sages' lives are actually true to how their doctrines should be interpreted. If you want more details about these matters, plenty of scholarly tomes are available to help confuse you further.

Though I call the great men and women I've described "sages," they were far from infallible. They were the products of their age, and some of their opinions—their social, religious or sexual values, for example—might strike many today as offensive. In regard to their understanding of physics and other sciences, sometimes they were right, sometimes they were wrong, and in other cases they were so far ahead of their times our scientists today still haven't caught up!

## The Continuing Quest

When I lecture around the country, the most frequent complaint I hear from audiences is that they're spiritually lonely. Their souls cry out for a more meaningful existence, for a life in which "spirit" is a living experience, not an empty word. But they have no one to share their yearning with. Their family members may be more interested in what's on TV that night than in seriously questioning the purpose of life. Friends may even mock them for attending meditation classes or bringing home a book on philosophy. Our Western culture generously feeds the body and mind, but it starves the soul.

If you feel this way, too, I'd like to remind you of a stunning story from the Bible (Matthew 12:46–49). The disciples tell Jesus his family has just arrived, but Jesus doesn't let them in. A little later his spiritual friends remind Jesus, "Your family is waiting outside."

Jesus answers, "Who is my family? *You* are my family."

The saints and sages and spiritual aspirants in this book are *your* family—your spiritual family. Spend more time with these people. They're good company.

# Index

# About the Author

LINDA JOHNSEN, M.S., is one of the most popular writers in the field of yoga and spirituality today. Her book *Daughters of the Goddess: The Women Saints of India* was voted "Best New Age Book of the Year" by the Midwest Book Association.

Linda is also author of *The Living Goddess: Reclaiming the Tradition of the Mother of the Universe*, *Meditation Is Boring?*, *A Thousand Suns*, *Teach Yourself Yoga*, *The Complete Idiot's Guide to Hinduism*, and *Kirtan: Chanting as a Spiritual Path*. She was a contributing editor for *Yoga + Joyful Living* magazine; her entertaining and enlightening essays have appeared in numerous magazines, journals, and anthologies. She has also appeared on radio and TV, while her lectures on the spiritual life have been enthusiastically embraced by audiences throughout the United States.

Linda earned a master's degree in Eastern Studies and Comparative Psychology at the University of Scranton's innovative program in yoga science and philosophy. She went on to do post-graduate work in Comparative Religions at the Graduate Theological Union in Berkeley. Linda is noted for uncovering fascinating true stories about the world's spiritual traditions known only to scholars, and explaining them to the rest of us in a way that is fascinating and extraordinarily inspiring. She lives in the San Francisco Bay Area with her husband, science educator Johnathan Brown.

## ABOUT ECKHART TOLLE EDITIONS

Eckhart Tolle Editions was launched in 2015 to publish life-changing works, both old and new, that have been personally selected by Eckhart Tolle. This imprint of New World Library presents books that can powerfully aid in transforming consciousness and awakening readers to a life of purpose and presence.

Learn more about Eckhart Tolle at

**www.eckharttolle.com**

**NEW WORLD LIBRARY** is dedicated to publishing books and other media that inspire and challenge us to improve the quality of our lives and the world.

We are a socially and environmentally aware company. We recognize that we have an ethical responsibility to our customers, our staff members, and our planet.

We serve our customers by creating the finest publications possible on personal growth, creativity, spirituality, wellness, and other areas of emerging importance. We serve New World Library employees with generous benefits, significant profit sharing, and constant encouragement to pursue their most expansive dreams.

As a member of the Green Press Initiative, we print an increasing number of books with soy-based ink on 100 percent postconsumer-waste recycled paper. Also, we power our offices with solar energy and contribute to nonprofit organizations working to make the world a better place for us all.

Our products are available in bookstores everywhere.

**www.newworldlibrary.com**

At NewWorldLibrary.com you can download our catalog, subscribe to our e-newsletter, read our blog, and link to authors' websites, videos, and podcasts.

Find us on Facebook, follow us on Twitter, and watch us on YouTube.

Send your questions and comments our way!
You make it possible for us to do what we love to do.

Phone: 415-884-2100 or 800-972-6657
Catalog requests: Ext. 10 | Orders: Ext. 10 | Fax: 415-884-2199
escort@newworldlibrary.com

NEW WORLD LIBRARY
*publishing books that change lives*                    14 Pamaron Way, Novato, CA 94949